LEANING INTO A HAIL OF BULLETS

LEANING INTO A HAIL OF BULLETS

REALLIFESTUFFFORMEN ON TEMPTATION

A BIBLE DISCUSSION GUIDE FEATURING

NAVPRESS®

BRINGING TRUTH TO LIFE

OUR GUARANTEE TO YOU

We believe so strongly in the message of our books that we are making this quality guarantee to you. If for any reason you are disappointed with the content of this book, return the title page to us with your name and address and we will refund to you the list price of the book. To help us serve you better, please briefly describe why you were disappointed. Mail your refund request to: NavPress, P.O. Box 35002, Colorado Springs, CO 80935.

The Navigators is an international Christian organization. Our mission is to reach, disciple, and equip people to know Christ and to make Him known through successive generations. We envision multitudes of diverse people in the United States and every other nation who have a passionate love for Christ, live a lifestyle of sharing Christ's love, and multiply spiritual laborers among those without Christ.

NavPress is the publishing ministry of The Navigators. NavPress publications help believers learn biblical truth and apply what they learn to their lives and ministries. Our mission is to stimulate spiritual formation among our readers.

ISBN 1-57683-690-8

Cover design by Arvid Wallen
Cover illustration by Jared Lee
Creative Team: Steve Parolini, Cara Iverson, Pat Miller

Written and compiled by Tim McLaughlin

Some of the anecdotal illustrations in this book are true to life and are included with the permission of the persons involved. All other illustrations are composites of real situations, and any resemblance to people living or dead is coincidental.

Unless otherwise identified, all Scripture quotations in this publication are taken from *THE MESSAGE* (MSG). Copyright © 1993, 1994, 1995, 1996, 2000, 2001, 2002. Used by permission of NavPress Publishing Group.

Printed in Canada

1 2 3 4 5 6 7 8 9 10 / 08 07 06 05 04

FOR A FREE CATALOG OF NAVPRESS BOOKS & BIBLE STUDIES,
CALL 1-800-366-7788 (USA) OR 1-416-499-4615 (CANADA)

CONTENTS

ABOUT THE
REALLIFESTUFFFORMEN
SERIES

Let your love dictate how you deal with me;
    teach me from your textbook on life.
I'm your servant—help me understand what that means,
    the inner meaning of your instructions. . . .
Break open your words, let the light shine out,
    let ordinary people see the meaning.

—PSALM 119:124-125,130

We're all yearning for understanding—for truth, wisdom, and hope. Whether we suffer in the simmering quiet of uncertainty or the megaphone cacophony of disbelief, we long for a better life—a more meaningful existence. We want to be Men Who Matter. But the fog of "real life stuff" we encounter every day obscures the life we crave, so we go on with the way things are.

Sometimes we pretend we don't care.

We do.

Sometimes we pretend everything is fine.

It isn't.

The truth is, the real life stuff matters. In that fog, there are things about our wives, our children, our friends, our work, and, most significantly, ourselves that cause varying degrees of distress, discomfort, and disease.

The REAL LIFE STUFF FOR MEN series is a safe place for exploring the truth about that fog. But it's not a typical Bible study. You won't find any fill-in-the-blank questions in these pages. Nor will you find any pat answers. It's likely you'll come away with more questions rather than fewer. But through personal reflection and—in a small group—lively discussion (the best part of a Bible study anyway), these books will take you where you *need* to go and bring greater hope and meaning to your life.

Each of the books in this series provides a place to ask the hard questions of yourself and others, a place to find comfort in the chaos, a place to enlarge understanding, and—with the guidance of the Holy Spirit—a place to discover Real Life Hope that brings meaning to the everyday.

INTRODUCTION

Don't be so naive and self-confident. You're not exempt. You could fall flat on your face as easily as anyone else. Forget about self-confidence; it's useless. Cultivate God-confidence.

No test or temptation that comes your way is beyond the course of what others have had to face. All you need to remember is that God will never let you down; he'll never let you be pushed past your limit; he'll always be there to help you come through it.

—1 Corinthians 10:12-13

Most of us need to be reminded that [Bible] stories are not exemplary in the sense that we stand back and admire them, like statues in a gallery, knowing all the while that we will never be able to live either that gloriously or tragically ourselves. Rather they are immersions into the actual business of living itself: this is what it means to be human. . . .

The biblical way is not so much to present us with a moral code and tell us "Live up to this"; nor is it to set out a system of doctrine and say, "Think like this and you will live well." The biblical way is to tell a story and invite us, "Live into this. This is what it looks like to be human; this is what is involved in entering and maturing as human beings."

—from the introduction to 1–2 Samuel, *The Message*

Part of being human is our frailty. We might as well get used to it. We are tempted, and as often as we resist, we give in, we slip, we fall, we backslide.

Some people seem hardwired to this or that temptation, whether by physiology or upbringing or whatever, and they spend their lives fighting it—sometimes successfully, sometimes not. Others suffer from the "It won't happen to me" syndrome, only to be eventually blind-sided and badly dented if not totaled by a temptation they never saw coming. This syndrome is particularly common among churched Christians, many of whom are taught, at least by implication, that they are indeed immune to some sins if they only do this, memorize that, just say no, or pledge their resistance.

Of course, if we learn anything from human nature, it is first that we remember precious little of our personal or our racial history; and second, that the very way to fall into a sin is to believe yourself impervious to it.

Naïve, you say? How could any man believe himself immune to sin?

Enter temptation, stage left. It is temptation that makes lying on a job or loan application seem suddenly like the only reasonable thing to do. It is temptation that scatters your common sense when a coworker touches your hand oh so briefly yet oh so significantly, and you go with that emotional flow instead of going home. It is temptation that eases you away from your rightful duties toward your family, friends, church, or boss.

If ever you wonder how you would *ever* sin in this or that way, just recall the last time you heard that a friend, celebrity, stranger, or relative tripped himself up in a serious way and you asked yourself, *Who would've thought?* Obviously, not you—and probably not him—but it happened.

Nor can you count on temptation being a temporary thing, maybe at your elbow or in your head for a season, but then conquered and gone. In some form or another, temptation is with us for life. Yet there is hope even in this, wrote the acutely self-observant C. S. Lewis in a letter:

I know about the despair of overcoming chronic temptation. It is not serious, provided self-offended petulance, annoyance at breaking records, impatience, etc. don't get the upper hand. No amount of falls will really undo us if we keep on picking ourselves up each time. We shall be very muddy and tattered children by the time we reach home.

But the bathrooms are all ready, the towels put out, and clean clothes in the airing cupboard. The only fatal thing is to lose one's temper and give it up. It is when we notice the dirt that God is most present in us; it is the very sign of his presence.[1]

Here's to talking with other men about your chronic temptations, here's to believing that God is rooting for you even when you succumb to temptation again and again, and here's to not giving up.

HOW TO USE THIS DISCUSSION GUIDE

This discussion guide is meant to be completed on your own and in a small group. So before you begin, line up a discussion group. Perhaps you already participate in a men's group. That works. Maybe you know a few friends who could do coffee once a week. That works, too. Ask around. You'll be surprised how many of your coworkers, team members, and neighbors would be interested in a small-group study—especially a study like this that doesn't require vast biblical knowledge. A group of four to six is optimal—any bigger and one or more members will likely be shut out of discussions. Your small group can also be two. Choose a friend who isn't afraid to "tell it like it is." Make sure each person has his own copy of the book.

1. *Read* the Scripture passages and other readings in each lesson on your own. Let it all soak in. Then use the white space provided to "think out loud on paper." Note content in the readings that troubles you, inspires you, confuses you, or challenges you. Be honest. Be bold. Don't shy away from the hard things. If you don't understand the passage, say so. If you don't agree, say that, too. You may choose to go over the material in one thirty- to forty-five-minute focused session. Or perhaps you'll spend twenty minutes a day on the readings.

2. *Think* about what you read. Think about what you wrote. Always ask, "What does this mean?" and "Why does this matter?" about

the readings. Compare different Bible translations. Respond to the questions we've provided. You may have a lot to say on one topic, little on another. That's okay. Come back to this when you're in your small group. Allow the experience of others to broaden your wisdom. You'll be stretched here—called upon to evaluate what you've discovered and asked to make practical sense of it. In community, that stretching can often be painful and sometimes even embarrassing. But your willingness to be transparent—your openness to the possibility of personal growth—will reap great rewards.

3. *Pray* as you go through the entire session: before you read a word, in the middle of your thinking process, when you get stuck on a concept or passage, and as you approach the time when you'll explore these passages and thoughts together in a small group. Pause when you need to ask God for inspiration or when you need to cry out in frustration. Speak your prayers, be silent, or use the prayer starter we've provided and write a prayer at the bottom of each page.

4. *Live.* (That's "live" as in "rhymes with give" as in "Give me something I can really use in my life.") Before you meet with your small group, complete as much of this section as you can (particularly the "What I Want to Discuss" section). Then, in your small group, ask the hard questions about what the lesson means to you. Dig deep for relevant, reachable goals. Record your real-world plan in the book. Commit to following through on these plans, and prepare to be held accountable.

5. *Follow up.* Don't let the life application drift away without action. Be accountable to small-group members and refer to previous "Live" as in "rhymes with give" sections often. Take time at the beginning of each new study to review. See how you're doing.

6. *Repeat* as necessary.

SMALL-GROUP STUDY TIPS

After going through each week's study on your own, it's time to sit down with others and go deeper. Here are a few thoughts on how to make the most of your small-group discussion time.

Set ground rules. You don't need many. Here are two:

First, you'll want group members to make a commitment to the entire eight-week study. A binding legal document with notarized signatures and commitments written in blood probably isn't necessary, but you know your friends best. Just remember this: Significant personal growth happens when group members spend enough time together to really get to know each other. Hit-and-miss attendance rarely allows this to occur.

Second, agree together that everyone's story is important. Time is a valuable commodity, so if you have an hour to spend together, do your best to give each person ample time to express concerns, pass along insights, and generally feel like a participating member of the group. Small-group discussions are not monologues. However, a one-person-dominated discussion isn't always a bad thing. Not only is your role in a small group to explore and expand your own understanding, it's also to support one another. If someone truly needs more of the floor, give it to him. There will be times when the needs of the one outweigh the needs of the many. Use good judgment and allow extra space when needed. *Your* time might be next week.

Meet regularly. Choose a time and place, and stick to it. No one likes showing up to Coffee Cupboard at 6:00 AM, only to discover the meeting was moved to Breakfast Barn at seven. Consistency removes stress that could otherwise frustrate discussion and subsequent personal growth. It's only eight weeks. You can do this.

Talk openly. If you enter this study with shields up, you're probably not alone. And you're not a "bad person" for your hesitation to unpack your life in front of friends or strangers. Maybe you're skeptical about the value of revealing the deepest parts of who you are to others. Maybe you're simply too afraid of what might fall out of the suitcase. You don't have to go to a place where you're uncomfortable. If you want to sit and listen, offer a few thoughts, or even express a surface level of your own pain, go ahead. But don't neglect what brings you to this place—that longing for meaning. You can't ignore it away. Dip your feet in the water of brutally honest discussion, and you may choose to dive in. There is healing here.

Stay on task. Refrain from sharing material that falls into the "too much information" category. Don't spill unnecessary stuff, such as your wife's penchant for midnight bedroom belly dancing or your boss's obsession with Jennifer Aniston. This is about discovering how you can be a better person.

If structure isn't your group's strength, try a few minutes of general comments about the study, and then take each "Live" question one at a time and give everyone in the group a chance to respond. That should get you into the meat of matters pretty quickly.

Hold each other accountable. That "Live" section is an important gear in the growth machine. If you're really ready for positive change—for spiritual growth—you'll want to take this section seriously. Not only should you personally be thorough as you summarize your discoveries, practical as you compose your goals, and realistic as you determine the plan for accountability, you must hold everyone else in the group accountable for doing these things. Be lovingly, brutally honest as you examine each other's "Live" section. Don't hold back—this is where the rubber meets the road. A lack of openness here may send other group members skidding off that road.

TEMPTATION TO RUN FROM TOUGH CIRCUMSTANCES

"Some days after work, the last thing I want to do is go home. I want to point the car in the opposite direction and just keep driving."

THE BEGINNING PLACE

You know you're not the first person in the world to want to run away from things—things like a hard stretch in your marriage, a job you dread facing every morning, financial pressures, relational pressures, professional pressures. You simply want out, and you're beginning to feel a little desperate about it.

The trouble is, you can't shake the feeling that fleeing is a coward's way out. If you had any emotional or spiritual backbone at all, you wouldn't feel like cutting and running. If you were mature, you'd stay with your hellish situation and slug it out or endure it or—like your grandparents, perhaps—make the best of it.

Think for a minute of who in the Bible did and didn't flee difficult circumstances. Who left town before they got themselves killed, and who hung in there, gutting it out with no guarantee of success?

- Jacob didn't face his twin brother's wrath after duping him and his blind father, Isaac, but instead fled from it all.
- Jonah didn't face an intimidating divine assignment but instead fled from God—or at least tried to.

• Jeremiah *did* hang in there during a desperate national and
political era—and he nearly hanged for it.

The apostle Paul seemed to have spent half his life fleeing assas-
sination or execution, and the other half *refusing to flee*, instead will-
ingly exposing himself to danger and trusting God for the outcome.

In this lesson, you'll explore what makes you feel like heading for
the hills and leaving it all behind, not that you feel like that every day.
But most men have spells now and then of wanting *out*—out of their
job, their marriage, their responsibilities. Then again, some men feel this
way most of their lives, whether or not they actually flee. How can you
deal with this temptation? Is there middle ground, where you can opt to
stay in miserable circumstances and yet glean a little joy in the process?

Use the space below to summarize your beginning place for this
lesson. Describe your realities as well as your desires about the temptation to flee—your marriage, your family, your job, whatever. We'll
start here and then go deeper.

READ Don't Jump

1 Peter 4:12-13,19

Friends, when life gets really difficult, don't jump to the conclusion that God isn't on the job. Instead, be glad that you are in the very thick of what Christ experienced. This is a spiritual refining process, with glory just around the corner. . . .

So if you find life difficult because you're doing what God said, take it in stride. Trust him. He knows what he's doing, and he'll keep on doing it.

THINK

- How do you explain hardship—the kind that begs you to run away from home, work, or a sphere of your life that you really care about? How directly is God's hand in it, if at all?
- What guarantees are there, if any, that you'll come through this hardship? That you'll be a better person because of it?
- Have you ever been in a crisis or hardship that you've wanted to flee and you can't see God's hand in it? Think about this.
- Describe a season of hardship you went through that made you want to flee but you ended up hanging in there. What made you hang in there?

PRAY

God, help me to see you . . .

READ   A Convenient Escape

From *The Divorce Dilemma*, by Richard Goodall[1]

In the days when divorce was not permitted, the reaction may well have been to put up with what had "gone wrong"; now that divorce is freely available, the reaction, first and foremost, is to escape. This is understandable, because any animal wishes to get out of a cage, no matter how beautiful and well furbished that cage may have been. The tragedy inherent in the situation is that one may leave a modern, clean and convenient type of prison and end up in a dungeon. . . .

It may almost sound trite but, if divorce were prohibited, people could not divorce. If people were not allowed to divorce, they would in some way or other find a *modus vivendi*, they would come to terms with each other's foibles, at least for the sake of the children. . . .

They all claim that they thought hard and long, as the expression goes, before taking such a serious step; that they were saddened once they decided that their marriages should terminate; that they were concerned for their children. Nevertheless, the decision had to be taken. The justification put forward always was along the lines that "it was my life that I had to think about," "you only live once and I could not continue living like that," and similar expressions which highlight the personal drama, which was genuinely felt, of the individual caught in the web of an unhappy marital relationship.

No criticism of such people is intended here. But the point needs to be restated that none of them put the wellbeing of their children first: in some form or other, for one reason or the other, each of them put their happiness first.

THINK

- Does it strike you as simplistic or realistic to argue that prohibiting divorce would make for a better society?

- If our society will not forbid divorce, can a couple? Or could a community or organization—such as a church, say—forbid divorce among couples who voluntarily submitted to the authority of said church or organization? What might be the benefits of such a social prohibition? Liabilities?
- In your observation or firsthand experience, how often is divorce a legally sanctioned way of fleeing a tough situation? How often is it a way of fleeing a toxic situation? Is there a difference?
- Is fleeing a tough or seemingly impossible marriage an essentially selfish act? Think about this.

PRAY

Lord, give me strength to . . .

READ   Facing Confusion

From *Dangers Men Face*, by Jerry White[2]

I was driving alone at night in Birmingham, England. I was lost. Perhaps not really lost, since I had some idea where I was. I recognized none of the street names. I couldn't tell if I was going towards or away from my destination.

I started down one street. After a mile I knew it was wrong. I went back to where I started and tried another route. I realized I was thoroughly confused. While I was trying to remember to drive on the left, to give way on the roundabouts, and generally not to do something stupid, I *felt* stupid. I knew I was close, but I was disoriented. After further trial and error, I finally arrived at my destination.

When I drive in a strange city, I know I will eventually figure out the right route, but the process of wrong turns, misjudgments, and confusing streets becomes very frustrating. I soon forget the new sights around me and become totally absorbed in finding my way.

Life is like that, often at the most inconvenient of times. One of the most disconcerting feelings a man can have is confusion. Men want to know where they are going and how to get there without asking for directions. Uncertainty troubles us. We want to be responsible and directed.

All men will face confusion at some point in their lives, probably at several points in their lives. Like many other dangers . . . confusion sneaks up and catches us unaware. We are traveling comfortably down a pathway and suddenly find the way obscured. A fog sets in and we cannot see clearly. Our thinking processes get muddled. Our ability to make decisions seems blocked. We are not just lost looking for the right road, we don't even know where we want to go.

THINK

- When have you experienced confusion that "sneaks up" on you? How did that confusion affect your decision-making ability? Were you tempted to simply not make a decision? Why or why not?
- How might uncertainty lead to a desire to abdicate responsibility?
- When decisions are difficult—due to your feeling "lost" or unsure—how can you move toward action that will resolve your lack of direction?
- When you're absorbed in trying to find your way, where can you turn to find help? What are the risks of not seeking help when you feel lost?

PRAY

Lord, show me how to . . .

READ As Far Away as You Can Get

Jonah 1:1-4

One day long ago, GOD's Word came to Jonah, Amittai's son: "Up on your feet and on your way to the big city of Nineveh! Preach to them. They're in a bad way and I can't ignore it any longer."

But Jonah got up and went the other direction to Tarshish, running away from GOD. He went down to the port of Joppa and found a ship headed for Tarshish. He paid the fare and went on board, joining those going to Tarshish—as far away from GOD as he could get.

But GOD sent a huge storm at sea, the waves towering.

THINK

- What do you remember about the first time you heard or read Jonah's story? What was your initial reaction to Jonah's decision to run away?
- Jonah's feelings triggered "a huge storm." What kind of storm did your situation cause?
- Have you reconciled God's difficult request with your disinclination to do it? Why or why not?
- What today is tempting you to "get out while you still can," though you know deep down you should stay and see it through to the end?

PRAY

Lord, give me wisdom to . . .

READ Go Back the Way You Came

1 Kings 19:1-15

[King] Ahab reported to [his queen] Jezebel everything that Elijah had done, including the massacre of the prophets. Jezebel immediately sent a messenger to Elijah with her threat: "The gods will get you for this and I'll get even with you! By this time tomorrow you'll be as dead as any one of those prophets."

When Elijah saw how things were, he ran for dear life to Beersheba, far in the south of Judah. He left his young servant there and then went on into the desert another day's journey. He came to a lone broom bush and collapsed in its shade, wanting in the worst way to be done with it all—to just die: "Enough of this, GOD! Take my life—I'm ready to join my ancestors in the grave!" Exhausted, he fell asleep under the lone broom bush.

Suddenly an angel shook him awake and said, "Get up and eat!"

He looked around and, to his surprise, right by his head were a loaf of bread baked on some coals and a jug of water. He ate the meal and went back to sleep.

The angel of GOD came back, shook him awake again, and said, "Get up and eat some more—you've got a long journey ahead of you."

He got up, ate and drank his fill, and set out. Nourished by that meal, he walked forty days and nights, all the way to the mountain of God, to Horeb. When he got there, he crawled into a cave and went to sleep.

Then the word of GOD came to him: "So Elijah, what are you doing here?"

"I've been working my heart out for the GOD-of-the-Angel-Armies," said Elijah. "The people of Israel have abandoned your covenant, destroyed the places of worship, and murdered your prophets. I'm the only one left, and now they're trying to kill me."

Then he was told, "Go, stand on the mountain at attention before GOD. GOD will pass by."

A hurricane wind ripped through the mountains and shat-tered the rocks before GOD, but GOD wasn't to be found in the wind; after the wind an earthquake, but GOD wasn't in the earth-quake; and after the earthquake fire, but GOD wasn't in the fire; and after the fire a gentle and quiet whisper.

When Elijah heard the quiet voice, he muffled his face with his great cloak, went to the mouth of the cave, and stood there. A quiet voice asked, "So Elijah, now tell me, what are you doing here?" Elijah said it again, "I've been working my heart out for GOD, the GOD-of-the-Angel-Armies, because the people of Israel have abandoned your covenant, destroyed your places of wor-ship, and murdered your prophets. I'm the only one left, and now they're trying to kill me."

GOD said, "Go back the way you came through the desert to Damascus."

THINK

- In what ways do you feel like Elijah?
- What was God's response to Elijah's fleeing for his life? What was God trying to tell the prophet with the wind, earthquake, fire, and whisper?
- What "voice" of God have you traditionally been most recep-tive to when you're tempted to flee or have fled? Does some-thing in you have to be shattered, shaken to the ground, or burned up before God has your attention?
- How do you feel about God making sure Elijah got enough food and rest during all his fleeing?
- What was God's last word to Elijah? Was this a word for just Elijah's specific situation, or might there be a word here for you, too?

THINK (CONTINUED)

PRAY

Father, help me to hear your voice . . .

READ Hanging In There

Job 1:8-12,20-22; 2:7-10; 3:1-3,11,23; 40:1-5

GOD said to Satan, "Have you noticed my friend Job? There's no one quite like him—honest and true to his word, totally devoted to God and hating evil."

Satan retorted, "So do you think Job does all that out of the sheer goodness of his heart? Why, no one ever had it so good! You pamper him like a pet, make sure nothing bad ever happens to him or his family or his possessions, bless everything he does—he can't lose!

"But what do you think would happen if you reached down and took away everything that is his? He'd curse you right to your face, that's what."

GOD replied, "We'll see. Go ahead—do what you want with all that is his. Just don't hurt *him*." . . .

[After the loss of his possessions and the deaths of his children,] Job got to his feet, ripped his robe, shaved his head, then fell to the ground and worshiped:

Naked I came from my mother's womb,
     naked I'll return to the womb of the earth.
GOD gives, GOD takes.
     God's name be ever blessed.

Not once through all this did Job sin; not once did he blame God. . . .

Job was ulcers and scabs from head to foot. They itched and oozed so badly that he took a piece of broken pottery to scrape himself, then went and sat on a trash heap, among the ashes.

His wife said, "Still holding on to your precious integrity, are you? Curse God and be done with it!"

He told her, "You're talking like an empty-headed fool. We take the good days from God—why not also the bad days?"

Not once through all this did Job sin. He said nothing against God. . . .

Then Job broke the silence. He spoke up and cursed his fate:

"Obliterate the day I was born.
    Blank out the night I was conceived! . . .
Why didn't I die at birth,
    my first breath out of the womb my last? . . .
What's the point of life when it doesn't make sense,
    when God blocks all the roads to meaning?" . . .

GOD then confronted Job directly:

"Now what do you have to say for yourself?
    Are you going to haul me, the Mighty One, into court and
    press charges?"

Job answered:

"I'm speechless, in awe—words fail me.
    I should never have opened my mouth!
I've talked too much, way too much.
    I'm ready to shut up and listen."

THINK

- If Jonah is the poster boy for fleeing tough circumstances, then Job wins the gold medal for hanging in there. Job embraced his tough circumstances. Describe a time in your past that you did the Job thing—that you hung in there in a tough situation.
- Job was tempted to do *spiritual* fleeing—blaming God and giving up. How is blaming God similar to abandoning tough circumstances?
- Job had lost all reason for living and even had wished he'd never been born. When you're tempted to duck out of critical, painful, or otherwise horrendous situations in your life, how

do you feel about the option of simply going through the motions until things begin to make sense again?

PRAY

God, give me courage to . . .

READ Infantile Indulgence

2 Timothy 2:10-13,22

That's why I stick it out here—so that everyone God calls will get in on the salvation of Christ in all its glory. This is a sure thing:

> If we die with him, we'll live with him;
> If we stick it out with him, we'll rule with him;
> If we turn our backs on him, he'll turn his back on us;
> If we give up on him, he does not give up—
>> for there's no way he can be false to himself. . . .

Run away from infantile indulgence. Run after mature righteousness—faith, love, peace—joining those who are in honest and serious prayer before God.

THINK

- Do Paul's words here seem like strong motivation to not flee from tough circumstances, or a harsh ultimatum for those thinking about fleeing? Or neither? Or both?
- According to the apostle, if you're going to flee, what is it you should flee from? And what should you flee toward?
- What does "infantile indulgence" look like to you?
- Who do you picture in your mind when you read "those who are in honest and serious prayer before God"? Could you, if you wanted to, realistically "flee" to them? How would they react?

THINK (CONTINUED)

PRAY

Father, I admit that I am . . .

LIVE

What I Want to Discuss

What have you discovered this week that you definitely want to discuss with your small group? Write that here. Then begin your small-group discussion with these thoughts.

So What?

Use the following space to summarize the truths you uncovered about responding to tough circumstances and what you really need to do to overcome the temptation to run. Review your "Beginning Place" if you need to remember where you began. How does God's truth impact the "next step" in your journey?

Then What?

What is one practical thing you can do to apply what you've discovered? Describe how you would put this into practice. What steps would you take? Remember to think realistically—an admirable but unreachable goal is as good as no goal. Discuss your goal in your small group to further define it.

How?

Identify how you will be held accountable to the goal you described. Who will be on your support team? What are their responsibilities? How will you measure the success of your plan? Write the details here.

TEMPTATION TO DRIFT FROM CHURCH

"It's not that I'm losing my faith or anything.
I've spent my life in church, and frankly, I need
a break—not from God, just from church."

A REMINDER:

Before you dive into this study, spend a little time reviewing what you wrote in the previous lesson's "Live" sections. How are you doing? Check with your small-group members and review your progress toward the specified goals. If necessary, adjust your goals and plans, and then recommit to them.

THE BEGINNING PLACE

It would be wise for church leaders to acknowledge what you've probably already noticed if you've spent any time at all in church: People attend church regularly for all sorts of reasons. Some go for the sermon. Others go in spite of the sermon. Others go for the worship. Still others attend in spite of the worship. Some attend for their children's sakes. Then there are those who are desperate; those who need fixing; those in the back pew who are merely curious; those who are personally fulfilled by volunteering, giving, and serving; those who want to perform musically on a regular basis; those who love to teach; those who are lifelong students; and so on.

The case could be made that all these reasons for going to church are legitimate. So which reasons are yours? Why do you go to church as often as you do?

Or do you go at all? Have the reasons you've been attending suddenly lost their influence? Are you tired of the church routine? More desirous of sleep than sermons? If you have been a regular churchgoer but have felt as though you're drifting away from church, perhaps this is a good time to consider why. What would the church need to do in order to overcome your temptation to skip? What would *you* need to do?

Use the space below to summarize your beginning place for this lesson. Describe your realities as well as your desires about any temptation you feel to drift away from church. We'll start here and then go deeper.

READ   Forced Attendance

From *Traveling Mercies*, by Anne Lamott[1]

Sam is the only kid he knows who goes to church—who is made to go to church two or three times a month. He rarely wants to. This is not exactly true: the truth is he *never* wants to go. What young boy would rather be in church on the weekends than hanging out with a friend? It does not help him to be reminded that once he's there he enjoys himself, that he gets to spend the time drawing in the little room outside the sanctuary, that he only actually has to sit still and listen during the short children's sermon.

You might think, noting the bitterness, the resignation, that he was being made to sit through a six-hour Latin mass. Or you might wonder why I make this strapping, exuberant boy come with me most weeks, and if you were to ask, this is what I would say.

I make him because I can. I outweigh him by nearly seventy-five pounds.

The main reason is that I want to give him what I found in the world, which is to say a path, a little light to see by. Most of the people I know who have what I want—which is to say, purpose, heart, balance, gratitude, joy—are people with a deep sense of spirituality. They are people in community, who pray, or practice their faith. They follow a brighter light than the glimmer of their own candle; they are part of something beautiful.

My relatives all live in the Bay Area and I adore them, but they are all as skittishly self-obsessed as I am, which I certainly mean in the nicest possible way. Let's just say that I do not leave family gatherings with the feeling that I have just received some kind of spiritual chemotherapy. But I do when I leave my little church.

THINK

- Granted, you're a man, not a boy, but are there any similarities you can pick out (with a degree of chagrin) between Sam and you?

- What did Lamott mean about following only the glimmer of one's own candle? What does that look like? What are its pleasures and perils?
- When's the last time you left church feeling as though you had "just received some kind of spiritual chemotherapy"? Or do you have a different way of putting it?
- Have you ever in your adulthood been required by a person, organization, or entity to go to church? What do you feel about that?

PRAY

God, help me to know the value of . . .

READ Spurring Each Other On

Hebrews 10:24-25

Let's see how inventive we can be in encouraging love and helping out, not avoiding worshiping together as some do but spurring
each other on, especially as we see the big Day approaching.

THINK

- List some ways you can "spur each other on" to "love and
  helping out." Do these ways all require your being at church?
  If not, then what's the big deal about church?
- How often do you hear the word *inventive* associated with
  church attendance? How might this concept rearrange your
  images of church, the possibilities of your involvement there?
- How motivating to you is the writer's comment that "the big
  Day" is approaching? How should this affect your resolve to
  worship together and spur each other on?

PRAY

Father, teach me to be inventive in . . .

READ   Here's the Church, Here's the Steeple . . .
Where Are All the People?

From the *Religion News Service* article "For Many Americans, Church Is Alien Territory," by Greg Garrison[2]

Church attendance has suffered a five-year decline and sunk to its lowest level in two decades, according to research by the Barna Research Group of Glendale, Calif.

"From the early '80s to the early '90s, there has been a definite change," said the Rev. Bruce Hose, who was director of Sunday school programs for the one-million-member Alabama Baptist Convention from 1985–1995. "Not only has attendance gone down but it is a graying culture, a graying congregation."

Hose said the Assemblies of God, Southern Baptists and some other denominations have continued to make membership gains, but much of the growth is focused in the megachurches.

In telephone surveys of 1,004 U.S. adults 18 and over, Barna Research Group said 37 percent of Americans now report going to church on a given Sunday. Attendance peaked in 1991 at 49 percent and dropped to 47 percent in 1992, 45 percent in 1993 and 42 percent in 1994 and 1995, according to the Barna poll numbers.

"Increasingly, we are seeing Christian churches lose entire segments of the population: men, singles, empty nesters . . . and people who were raised in mainline Protestant churches," wrote pollster George Barna.

"If his poll data is right, it's even worse than what we think we have found," said Samford University researcher Penny Long Marler, who has taken part in studies that have shown that actual church attendance is only about half of that indicated by telephone polls. "It may be where we're heading."

THINK

- At this point in your life, are you part of the church-attendance loss, or are you among those who have recently started attending or returned to church? What drew you to that decision?

- What demographic slices mentioned in this article—single, empty nester, boomer, mainline Protestant—represent you? Has your church attendance dropped off? Why or why not?
- What roles do spiritual apathy and ineffective churches play in declining attendance?

PRAY

Lord, help me to make a commitment to . . .

READ Why Attend?

1 Corinthians 14:26

> So here's what I want you to do. When you gather for worship,
> each one of you be prepared with something that will be useful
> for all: Sing a hymn, teach a lesson, tell a story, lead a prayer,
> provide an insight.

1 Corinthians 12:13-14,18,25-26

> By means of [God's] one Spirit, we all said goodbye to our partial
> and piecemeal lives. We each used to independently call our
> own shots, but then we entered into a large and integrated life in
> which he has the final say in everything. (This is what we pro-
> claimed in word and action when we were baptized.) Each of us
> is now a part of his resurrection body, refreshed and sustained at
> one fountain—his Spirit—where we all come to drink. The old
> labels we once used to identify ourselves—labels like Jew or
> Greek, slave or free—are no longer useful. We need something
> larger, more comprehensive.
>
> I want you to think about how all this makes you more sig-
> nificant, not less. A body isn't just a single part blown up into
> something huge. It's all the different-but-similar parts arranged
> and functioning together. . . . As it is, we see that God has care-
> fully placed each part of the body right where he wanted it. . . .
>
> The way God designed our bodies is a model for under-
> standing our lives together as a church: every part dependent on
> every other part, the parts we mention and the parts we don't,
> the parts we see and the parts we don't. If one part hurts, every
> other part is involved in the hurt, and in the healing. If one part
> flourishes, every other part enters into the exuberance.

THINK

- Judging from these New Testament words to the Corinthians, what does the apostle think seems to be the prime reason for attending church?
- Why do you go to church? Or why *did* you go, or why *would* you go?
- What does Paul have to say to one's protest of "But I can't teach or sing or direct a program at church"?
- To what degree might there be a touch of arrogance in a person who holds himself back from regularly mingling with other Christians?

PRAY

God, clarify my confusion about . . .

READ   Social Capital

From an interview with Robert D. Putnam, author of *Bowling Alone*[3]

For the past several years your work has focused on the importance of what you call "social capital." Why is it so important?

Social networks have amazing powers. People who are more connected with other people live longer and are healthier. In communities where people are connected, the schools work better, the crime rate is lower, the economic growth rate is higher. The power of social networks is a remarkable discovery of social science over the past decade or two.

About a decade ago I began to wonder about the trends in social capital in America. Historically, Americans, compared to people in other places, have connected with one another a lot. As a result, we've had very high levels of social capital. But in the last 30 years of the 20th century, for some reason or set of reasons, we began to be much less connected with our friends and neighbors and communities and churches.

The number of people who say that they belong to churches is down. And philanthropy is down. Giving, as a fraction of our income, rose for most of the 20th century and then began to decline in the last decades of the century. The peak of our generosity as a fraction of our income nationwide was in 1965. By almost every measure, Americans have become much less connected.

Does this finding refer only to formal group membership, or does it also describe what's happening to more informal ways of connecting?

Even informal ways are affected. For example, there's been a 60 percent decline in the number of picnics, and we spend less time having dinner with our families. Also, we don't trust other people as much.

I don't think the statistical evidence is surprising. What I think is surprising is how sharp and pervasive this decline has been.

What caused the decline of social capital?

There is no single cause. One of the culprits is television. Television watching is lethal for social connectiveness. Another part of the problem is the rise of two-career families. As women moved into the paid labor force, they have had less time for doing the things that build social capital. Men have not picked up the slack. And there's been a real loss in the time that people have for family and community obligations.

I want to make it clear that women are not to blame in all this. The fault is with all of us who have not adjusted to that overdue change in gender equality.

Another part of the problem is urban sprawl. Every ten minutes more of additional commuting time cuts all forms of social connection by 10 percent. So 10 percent more commuting time means 10 percent less churchgoing, 10 percent fewer PTA meetings and so on.

Finally, there may have been a kind of a cultural change in the 1960s that caused people to value self-interests and self-concerns and to be less connected with their communities.

Proverbs 27:17

You use steel to sharpen steel,
    and one friend sharpens another.

THINK

- What do you remember of "social capital" during your childhood? What connections did you and your family have with your community?
- What role did church play in your childhood? How has that role (or its absence) affected your adult churchgoing habits (or lack of them)?
- Do you feel that the world—or at least *your* world—is becoming more self-centered? Or that churches aren't staying

relevant to shifting cultural realities? Think about this.

• Respond to the following statement: "Just as you can't sharpen a blade without rubbing it up against something else, you won't keep your spiritual edge without rubbing up against other Christians in worship, in prayer, in service together—in short, at church."

PRAY

Lord, give me wisdom to . . .

READ A Daily Discipline

Acts 2:41-47

That day about three thousand took him at his word, were baptized and were signed up. They committed themselves to the teaching of the apostles, the life together, the common meal, and the prayers.

Everyone around was in awe—all those wonders and signs done through the apostles! And all the believers lived in a wonderful harmony, holding everything in common. They sold whatever they owned and pooled their resources so that each person's need was met.

They followed a daily discipline of worship in the Temple followed by meals at home, every meal a celebration, exuberant and joyful, as they praised God. People in general liked what they saw. Every day their number grew as God added those who were saved.

1 Corinthians 1:10

I have a serious concern to bring up with you, my friends, using the authority of Jesus, our Master. I'll put it as urgently as I can: You must get along with each other. You must learn to be considerate of one another, cultivating a life in common.

THINK

- What were several distinctive traits of the early church, according to Luke's account in Acts?
- List the differences and similarities between your church today and the early church as Luke described it in Acts.
- Notice how ritual worship and communalism seemed joined at the hip in the early church. What would this look like today, in your church?

- What are one or two ways you can overcome any temptation you might feel to withdraw from church and, in Paul's words, "cultivate a life in common"?

PRAY

Father, help me discover from church that . . .

READ   When You Gather

Matthew 18:19-20

> "When two of you get together on anything at all on earth and make a prayer of it, my Father in heaven goes into action. And when two or three of you are together because of me, you can be sure that I'll be there."

THINK

- What is the promise here, if any? Do you have any personal evidence supporting or contradicting such a promise?
- How comfortable are you with a literal understanding of these words of Jesus? For example, can *one* Christian expect any action on his prayers? Do more people gathered because of Jesus mean more God-action?
- What would you say to someone who told you, "There's just something about community. Some matters of faith, around faith, through faith, into faith—some of these matters just weren't made to be done solo"?

PRAY

Lord, thank you for the promise of . . .

LIVE

What I Want to Discuss

What have you discovered this week that you definitely want to discuss with your small group? Write that here. Then begin your small-group discussion with these thoughts.

So What?

Use the following space to summarize the truths you uncovered about your commitment to and understanding of church and what you really need to do to overcome the temptation to drift away. Review your "Beginning Place" if you need to remember where you began. How does God's truth impact the "next step" in your journey?

Then What?

What is one practical thing you can do to apply what you've discovered? Describe how you would put this into practice. What steps would you take? Remember to think realistically—an admirable but unreachable goal is as good as no goal. Discuss your goal in your small group to further define it.

How?

Identify how you will be held accountable to the goal you described. Who will be on your support team? What are their responsibilities? How will you measure the success of your plan? Write the details here.

TEMPTATION TO FUDGE ON FINANCIALS

"Look, with corporations evading millions in taxes, what's the practical difference between their loopholes and the few dollars I can keep from the IRS each year?"

A REMINDER:

Before you dive into this study, spend a little time reviewing what you wrote in the previous lesson's "Live" sections. How are you doing? Check with your small-group members and review your progress toward the specified goals. If necessary, adjust your goals and plans, and then recommit to them.

THE BEGINNING PLACE

There are three things, it is said, you steer clear of in conversation if you value your friends: sex, religion, and politics.

So much for *that* old saw. All three get plenty of airtime now—in the media, in chitchat among strangers, in fervent conversation between intimates—leaving the state of your personal finances as perhaps the only conversation subject most people tiptoe around. How much you earn, how much you owe, the sum of your assets or your liabilities— when these questions come up, answers become vague in a hurry.

If the Bible is any indication, God is a bull in a china shop when it comes to any of these—sex, religion, politics, or money. He has an opinion on all of them—even on your taxes, even when you can ill afford to pay them, even when you have doubts about how they're levied or how they're used.

For as little attention as Jesus paid to his own personal bank account, he seemed always to keep away the creditors. In the middle of ministry, for example, he instructed Peter to "go down to the lake, cast a hook, and pull in the first fish that bites. Open its mouth and you'll find a coin. Take it and give it to the tax men. It will be enough for both of us" (Matthew 17:27).

So where are the supernatural fish when you need them? Good question. In fact, there are *lots* of good questions when it comes to mixing personal finances with living as a Christian. Temptations abound when it comes to accounting for what you spend in a given year, what deductions you itemize, and how you itemize them. At what point does taking advantage of a tax loophole become cheating?

Use the space below to summarize your beginning place for this lesson. Describe your realities as well as your desires about temptations to fudge on financials. We'll start here and then go deeper.

READ Taxing Questions

From the beliefnet.com online poll "Is It OK to Cheat on Your Taxes?"[1]

You've slaved over the fine print, scribbled calculations, and tested your faith in Uncle Sam. Now what do you believe about your taxes? Take this completely anonymous, completely arbitrary set of polls below and see what others believe.

1. How are you most likely to cheat on your taxes?
   a. Fail to include all income
   b. Claim a family car as a company vehicle
   c. Pad your charitable deductions
   d. Deduct dinner with friend as a business meal

2. Everyone knows waiters, for instance, don't report all their tips. Should we raise tax rates on cash income to compensate for underreporting?
   a. Yes, what a clever idea.
   b. No, it would punish those who follow the rules.
   c. No, high tax rates already encourage underreporting.

3. If I suspected my spouse were cutting corners on taxes, I would:
   a. Call him or her on it. I have to sign the return, too.
   b. Let it go.
   c. Decide to do the same.

4. Is exploiting a loophole—like creating trusts for people you never met—cheating?
   a. No. Loopholes are built into the system.
   b. Yes. It's against the spirit of the law and only available to rich people.

5. You give the Salvation Army a bag of old clothes. New, the clothes cost $600. What do you deduct?
   a. $300
   b. $400

    c. $600
    d. $1,200

  6. Tax evasion is an act most comparable to:
    a. Speeding
    b. Burning the flag
    c. Perjury
    d. Treason

THINK

- There is no scoring table for this poll, but how would you score your own responses? What would a "good score" really mean?
- What responses other than those listed would most accurately reflect your perspective?
- Which of these questions (if any) made you wince most?
- What did you learn about yourself by taking this poll? What drives people (Christians and nonChristians alike) to "fudge" in financial matters?

PRAY

Lord, I need help to . . .

READ Citizen Pain

Romans 13:1-7

Be a good citizen. All governments are under God. Insofar as there is peace and order, it's God's order. So live responsibly as a citizen. If you're irresponsible to the state, then you're irresponsible with God, and God will hold you responsible. Duly constituted authorities are only a threat if you're trying to get by with something. Decent citizens should have nothing to fear.

Do you want to be on good terms with the government? Be a responsible citizen and you'll get on just fine, the government working to your advantage. But if you're breaking the rules right and left, watch out. The police aren't there just to be admired in their uniforms. God also has an interest in keeping order, and he uses them to do it. That's why you must live responsibly—not just to avoid punishment but also because it's the right way to live.

That's also why you pay taxes—so that an orderly way of life can be maintained. Fulfill your obligations as a citizen. Pay your taxes, pay your bills, respect your leaders.

THINK

- Christians were persecuted as often for sacrilege against the pantheon of Roman gods as for anything else, hence Paul's urging to be "good" citizens. It worked, too. Christians were some of the best citizens Rome had. Does the modern world share any of these characteristics? Describe them.
- If you're a "bad citizen," does that make you a "bad Christian" as well? What do you think Paul is saying about this?
- Remember the founding fathers of America and their fight against British governance? Imagine a conversation between Paul of Tarsus and Franklin of Philadelphia. How would they answer each other's points and objections?

- Does the reality of oppressive governments, corrupt police forces, and excessive tax rates make Paul's words here untrue? How, if at all, do you factor reality into this teaching?

PRAY

God, help me to be a good citizen by . . .

READ   Cutting Corners

2 Chronicles 25:6-10

[Amaziah] hired 100,000 soldiers from Israel in the north at a cost of about four and a half tons of silver.

A holy man showed up and said, "No, O king—don't let those northern Israelite soldiers into your army; GOD is not on their side, nor with any of the Ephraimites. Instead, you go by yourself and be strong. God and God only has the power to help or hurt your cause."

But Amaziah said to the holy man, "But what about all this money—these tons of silver I have already paid out to hire these men?"

"GOD's help is worth far more to you than that," said the holy man.

So Amaziah fired the soldiers he had hired from the north and sent them home. They were very angry at losing their jobs and went home seething.

THINK

- When was the last time you were tempted like Amaziah—feeling that you had to buy security or else suffer dire consequences?
- From your experience, fill in the blank: "God's help is worth far more to me than _____."
- It took a prophet to remind Amaziah that fundamentally it's God, not money, who saves us from the Canaanites or the creditors. Has there ever been such a "prophet" in your life? What were the circumstances that prompted this person's guidance?
- Have you ever given in to the temptation to fudge on your financials, failing to see God's help materialize in the way you hoped or expected? Explain.

THINK (CONTINUED)

PRAY

Father, give me strength to . . .

READ The Likelihood of Getting Caught

From the BookkeeperList.com article "Cheating on Taxes? Really?!" [2]

It shouldn't come as a shock to hear it's a crime to cheat on your taxes. In a recent year, however, only 2,472 Americans were convicted of tax crimes—.0022 percent of all taxpayers. This number is astonishingly small, taking into account the fact that the IRS estimates that 17 percent of all taxpayers are not complying with the tax laws. And the number of convictions for tax crimes has decreased over the past decade.

According to the IRS, individual taxpayers do 75 percent of the cheating—mostly middle-income earners. Corporations do most of the rest. Cash-intensive businesses and service-industry workers, from handy-people to doctors, are the worst offenders. For example, the IRS claims that waiters and waitresses underreport their cash tips by an average of 84 percent.

Most people cheat by deliberately underreporting income. A government study found the bulk of the underreporting of income was done by self-employed restaurateurs, clothing-store owners and—you'll no doubt be shocked—car dealers. Telemarketers and salespeople came in next, followed by doctors, lawyers (heavens!), accountants (heavens again!), and hairdressers.

Self-employed taxpayers who over-deduct business-related expenses—such as car expenses—came in a distant second on the cheaters hit parade. Surprisingly, the IRS has concluded that only 6.8 percent of deductions are overstated or just plain phony.

THINK

- How does the unlikelihood of being caught affect how scrupulous you are in doing your taxes?
- Is it surprising to you that individual taxpayers, not corporations, are responsible for most of the cheating? In what ways do individuals rationalize cheating? How is that any different from corporation loopholes?

- Which kinds of cheating mentioned in this excerpt are you most inclined to stumble into or indulge in? What are the gray areas for you?
- Do you believe Jesus wants you to obey the letter of your government's tax law, or the spirit of it? Explain.

PRAY

Father, I need wisdom to . . .

READ   The Government of "They"

From the *Money* article "We're Cheating One Another," by Frank Lalli[3]

You would hope that a clerk of a state supreme court would have more respect for the law and for his country. Not this guy. He was more than willing to tell a *Money* reporter how he had cheated on his income taxes for five years by taking a personal exemption ($2,050 in 1990) for a son who never existed. "Alex is a nice little kid," he joked. "He's real quiet, never bothered me, and he saved me $400 a year in taxes. That was my life of crime."

Only he doesn't consider what he did a crime. "I recognize the criminal implications, sure," he said. "But I was more than prepared to go to the judge and explain my reasons." The big one: he doesn't respect our government. He refers to the government as "they," and adds, "They're out to take as much money as they can from you." . . .

That court clerk with the fictitious kid and many others like him try to justify their dishonesty by denigrating their responsibilities as citizens. They dismiss the government as an amoral abstraction by calling it "they," as in: "They haven't served me, so why should I pay them?" Whenever you run into those people—at your office, over drinks or in your own living room—they need to be told that the government is not a "they." It is we, the people.

THINK

- Should respect for government play into your decision to pay taxes? Why or why not?
- When (if ever) have you fallen into the trap of referring to the government as "they"? What prompted that sort of thinking?
- In what ways does the temptation to cheat on taxes reduce the government to "an amoral abstraction"?

THINK (CONTINUED)

PRAY

God, give me direction so . . .

READ Render unto Caesar

Mark 12:13-17

They sent some Pharisees and followers of Herod to bait him, hoping to catch him saying something incriminating. They came up and said, "Teacher, we know you have integrity, that you are indifferent to public opinion, don't pander to your students, and teach the way of God accurately. Tell us: Is it lawful to pay taxes to Caesar or not?"

He knew it was a trick question, and said, "Why are you playing these games with me? Bring me a coin and let me look at it." They handed him one.

"This engraving—who does it look like? And whose name is on it?"

"Caesar," they said.

Jesus said, "Give Caesar what is his, and give God what is his." Their mouths hung open, speechless.

Adapted from the beliefnet.com online article "What Belongs to God?" by Marcus Borg [4]

Jesus' famous "render unto Caesar" saying flummoxed his opponents and leaves today's Christians scratching their heads.

Over the centuries, many Christians have based their attitudes toward government on this passage. Some have thought that Jesus' statement establishes two separate realms, Caesar's and God's, and that people should render to each what they ask for in their respective realms. This interpretation strikes many Americans as obviously correct, given our separation of church and state.

Yet in their historical context, these words of Jesus had little to do with taxation or political authority in general. Jews in the first century paid several taxes: tithes to the temple (averaging about 21 percent a year), customs taxes, and taxes on land. The people identified as Jesus' opponents were not questioning taxes in general. Their question was more specific: "Is it lawful to pay taxes to Caesar?"

The tax in question was the annual tribute tax to Rome. Jews were divided about this tax. The temple authorities and their retainers (including temple scribes) collaborated with Roman rule and endorsed the tax. But Jews sympathetic to the resistance to Roman authority rejected it. Such refusal was the equivalent of sedition.

The question put to Jesus was a trap. Either a yes or no answer would have gotten Jesus in trouble. "Yes" would have discredited him with those who found the imperial domination system reprehensible and unacceptable. "No" would have made him subject to arrest for sedition.

Jesus avoided the trap with two moves. First, he asked his opponents for a coin. When they produced one, Jesus looked at it and asked, "Whose image and inscription is this?"

It was, of course, an image of Caesar (presumably of Tiberius, the current Caesar). Moreover, its inscription heralded Tiberius as "son of the divine Augustus" (that is, son of a divine being) and would have been offensive to many Jews.

The coin bearing Caesar's image set up Jesus' second move, the famous saying itself: "Render to Caesar the things that are Caesar's, and to God the things that are God's."

In context, the saying is thoroughly ambiguous. The word "render" means "give back." The first half of the saying could thus mean, "It's Caesar's coin—go ahead and give it back to him." We can imagine Jesus saying this with a dismissive shrug. Rather than a pronouncement about the legitimacy of Roman imperial rule or political authority in general, his words might very well have been a brilliant way of evading the trap.

When its second half is added, the phrase remains equally ambiguous. What belongs to Caesar, and what belongs to God? The possible answers range from "Pay your tribute tax to Caesar, and your temple tax to God" to "Everything belongs to God." If the latter, what is owed to Caesar? Nothing. But the text itself provides no clue as to what was meant.

Jesus responded in a deliberately enigmatic way in order to avoid the trap set by his opponents. His response was never meant to be figured out. Rather, in this passage as in several others, we see his deft debating skill.

Thus this text offers little or no guidance for tax season. It neither claims taxation is legitimate nor gives aid to antitax activists.

THINK

- Do you agree with the theologian's interpretation of this passage? Why or why not?
- Some days you hear, "Give Caesar what is his, and give God what is his." Other days you hear, "It's all God's—your life, your time, your money." Can both be true, and if so, how do you know what the circumstances call for day to day?
- If it's God's money, is it possible you owe it not only to the government but also to organizations, groups, or individuals who help needy people more directly? What implications does this have for your finances?

PRAY

Lord, help me to know . . .

READ   Keeping an Honest Shop

Psalm 26

Clear my name, GOD;
    I've kept an honest shop.
I've thrown in my lot with you, GOD, and
    I'm not budging.

Examine me, GOD, from head to foot,
    order your battery of tests.
Make sure I'm fit
    inside and out

So I never lose
    sight of your love,
But keep in step with you,
    never missing a beat.

I don't hang out with tricksters,
    I don't pal around with thugs;
I hate that pack of gangsters,
    I don't deal with double-dealers.

I scrub my hands with purest soap,
    then join hands with the others in the great circle,
    dancing around your altar, GOD,
Singing God-songs at the top of my lungs,
    telling God-stories.

GOD, I love living with you;
    your house glows with your glory.
When it's time for spring cleaning,
    don't sweep me out with the quacks and crooks,
Men with bags of dirty tricks,
    women with purses stuffed with bribe-money.

You know I've been aboveboard with you;
    now be aboveboard with me.

I'm on the level with you, GOD;
>   I bless you every chance I get.

THINK

- From this passage, what can you learn about being brutally honest with God?
- What in your financial dealings tempts you in such a way that, were you to give in to this temptation, you could not tell God, "I've kept an honest shop"?
- David seems to make a close connection between *worship* and *practical honesty*. How are these elements related in your life?
- What if anything needs sweeping out before you can say, "You know, God, I've been aboveboard with you"?

PRAY

Father, help me to be honest about . . .

LIVE

What I Want to Discuss

What have you discovered this week that you definitely want to discuss with your small group? Write that here. Then begin your small-group discussion with these thoughts.

So What?

Use the following space to summarize the truths you uncovered about the temptation to fudge on financials and what you really need to do to overcome that temptation. Review your "Beginning Place" if you need to remember where you began. How does God's truth impact the "next step" in your journey?

Then What?

What is one practical thing you can do to apply what you've discovered? Describe how you would put this into practice. What steps would you take? Remember to think realistically—an admirable but unreachable goal is as good as no goal. Discuss your goal in your small group to further define it.

How?

Identify how you will be held accountable to the goal you described. Who will be on your support team? What are their responsibilities? How will you measure the success of your plan? Write the details here.

TEMPTATION TO FOLLOW LUSTFUL THOUGHTS

"I'm only human. I mean, I don't go out of my way to find those Internet sites. Besides, I don't act out; I don't do sinful acts. It's just curiosity."

A REMINDER:

Before you dive into this study, spend a little time reviewing what you wrote in the previous lesson's "Live" sections. How are you doing? Check with your small-group members and review your progress toward the specified goals. If necessary, adjust your goals and plans, and then recommit to them.

THE BEGINNING PLACE

If it were all so simple! If only there were evil people somewhere insidiously committing evil deeds, and it were necessary only to separate them from the rest of us and destroy them. But the line dividing good and evil cuts through the heart of every human being. And who is willing to destroy a piece of his own heart?

—Aleksandr Solzhenitsyn, *The Gulag Archipelago*

For all that we yearn to live "a life of purity," to have a clear conscience, and to enjoy an inner life that fantasizes more on the goodness of God than on the sleek bodies in our offices or on the Internet—for all that we want this, our minds are divided. Our devotion to wives or fiancées coexists uncomfortably with the urge to rubberneck a pair of exquisite legs that passes our desk, to linger on a random pop-up ad, to imagine what it'd be like to make love to our neighbor or our sister-in-law or that cute little rep who makes it very clear how much she enjoys the business lunches we share once a month. The line dividing good and evil cuts through our own heart indeed, though we are Christians, though we are redeemed by the blood of Jesus, though our heart's desire is to think and behave better than we do.

The world does little to strengthen our resolve, and seemingly everything to destroy it. America has a self-righteous spasm when a bare breast is flashed during a Super Bowl halftime musical show, but what about the lyrics to any of the songs performed that evening? Where is the corresponding outrage about misogynistic rap, about the sexual tease used to sell movies about high schoolers to high schoolers? About the overt, mainstream, and public references to sexual details once kept inside closed bedroom doors?

Our economy profits from instant gratification, whether it's chewing gum at the checkout line or phone-sex services. It's so pervasive; you probably can't fight it alone. So find some male friends in whom you can confide, and resolve to fight this thing together.

This lesson explores the temptations of lust, of fantasizing, and of pornography, and of how to face it (so to speak), deal with it, and deliver yourself from it. Use the space below to summarize your beginning place for this lesson. Describe your own realities about lust, whether it takes the form of fantasizing, Internet or print porn, or acting out. Describe also where you want your head and heart in this matter. We'll start here and then go deeper.

READ   Under Lust's Command

Isaiah 9:18-20

> Their wicked lives raged like an out-of-control fire,
>   the kind that burns everything in its path—
> Trees and bushes, weeds and grasses—
>   filling the skies with smoke.
> GOD-of-the-Angel-Armies answered fire with fire,
>   set the whole country on fire,
> Turned the people into consuming fires,
>   consuming one another in their lusts—
> Appetites insatiable, stuffing and gorging
>   themselves left and right with people and things.
> But still they starved. Not even their children
>   were safe from their rapacious hunger.

From Dante's *Inferno*, canto 5[1]

> I came to a place where light was absent,
> A place which bellowed like a stormy sea when
> Clashing winds whip it into torment.
>
> The infernal hurricane, which can never slacken,
> Drives the spirits with its violence;
> Whirling and lashing, it leaves them beaten.
>
> Swept back before their place of sentence,
> The spirits shriek, moan, lament, and
> Curse the divine power with vehemence.
> I learned that those condemned to this brand
> Of torture are called carnal sinners,
> Those who put reason under lust's command.
>
> And just as starlings in cold winters
> Are borne by their wings in large, crowded flocks,
> So by this blast are these evil gliders.

Now here, now there, now up, now down the wind knocks
These shades, with no hope of either rest
Or relief from pain, so cruelly it mocks.

THINK

- What in Dante's vision is the one obvious characteristic of that part of hell where "carnal sinners, those who put reason under lust's command" are punished?
- How appropriate to you are fire and wind as symbols of lust? Explain.
- When in your life have you felt an insatiable appetite for something or someone—or when have you felt blown out of control by the winds of your own passion?
- Whether or not you have faced such extreme lust as the prophet and the poet describe here, how would you describe the lust you *have* felt?

PRAY

Lord, forgive me for . . .

READ The Temptation That Won't Go Away

From the *Christianity Today* editorial "We've Got Porn"[2]

Survey results showed that one in four American men (25.9%) and about one in six women (16.7%) say it is either very or somewhat likely they can find sexual fulfillment online. Nearly one in five Christians (18.68%) gives the same response.

THINK

- How do you account for the fact that Christians are nearly as inclined as the general public to "find sexual fulfillment online"?
- What if anything does this statistic say to you about churches? About *your* church?
- Which of the following has been your approach: to simply live with the reality of porn and find ways to deal with it, or to remove yourself altogether from the potential influence of porn?
- How can a man keep himself protected from the influence of porn? Is this even a realistic aim anymore? If not, what *is* a realistic goal?

PRAY

Father, guide me to . . .

READ The Damage

From the *Washington Times* article "Looking Beyond Lust," by Emily Louise Zimbrick[3]

To men accustomed to watching the extreme action of porn stars, ordinary sex may "barely register on the thrill scale," feminist author Naomi Wolf wrote in the October 2003 issue of *New York* magazine. And pornography creates new expectations of beauty for women, she says. "Being naked is not enough; you have to be buff, be tan with no tan lines, have the surgically hoisted breasts and the Brazilian bikini wax—just like porn stars. . . . Pornography is addictive; the baseline gets ratcheted up."

From the *Time* article "The Porn Factor," by Pamela Paul[4]

In a *Friends* episode titled "The One with Free Porn," Chandler and Joey discover to their delight a free pornography TV channel, which they leave on and watch endlessly for fear it will go away. Later, a startled Chandler reports to Joey, "I was just at the bank, and there was this really hot teller, and she didn't ask me to go do it in the vault." Joey describes a similar cold shoulder from the pizza-delivery woman. "You know what?" Chandler concludes. "We have to turn off the porn."

Chandler may be on to something. Call it the porn factor. Whereas pornography was once furtively glimpsed at dimly lighted newsstands or seedy adult theaters, today it is everywhere. It pours in over the Internet, sometimes uninvited, sometimes via eagerly forwarded links (Paris Hilton, anyone?). It titillates 24/7 on steamy adult cable channels and on-demand services (the pay-per-view reality show *Can You Be a Porn Star?* made its debut this month). It has infiltrated mainstream cable with HBO's forthcoming documentary series *Pornucopia: Going Down in the Valley.* And in ways that have only begun to be measured, it is coloring relationships, both long- and short-term, reshaping expectations about sex and body image and, most worrisome of all, threatening to alter how young people learn about sex.

In recent years, a number of psychologists and sociologists have joined the chorus of religious and political opponents in warning about the impact of pervasive pornography. They argue that porn is transforming sexuality and relationships—for the worse. Experts say men who frequently view porn may develop unrealistic expectations of women's appearance and behavior, and have difficulty forming and sustaining relationships and feeling sexually satisfied. Fueled by a combination of access, anonymity and affordability, online porn has catapulted overall pornography consumption—bringing in new viewers, encouraging more use from existing fans and escalating consumers from soft-core to harder-core material. Cyberporn is even giving rise to a new form of sexual compulsiveness. According to Alvin Cooper, who conducts seminars on cybersex addiction, 15% of online-porn habitues develop sexual behavior that disrupts their lives. "The Internet is the crack cocaine of sexual addiction," says Jennifer Schneider, co-author of *Cybersex Exposed: Simple Fantasy or Obsession?*

THINK

- Describe the first time you noticed that your wife (fiancée, long-time girlfriend) had dropped considerably on the "thrill scale."
- Where did you get your expectations about how a woman should look? About how she should respond to you in public, around the house, in bed?
- Respond to the following quote: "Experts say men who frequently view porn may develop unrealistic expectations of women's appearance and behavior, have difficulty forming and sustaining relationships and feeling sexually satisfied."
- Do you agree that the Internet is the "crack cocaine of sexual addiction"? As with alcohol, do you believe that different men have different thresholds of resistance to porn? Why or why not? How are you dealing with this temptation?

THINK (CONTINUED)

.

PRAY

God, help me to avoid . . .

READ   Where Is Your Line?

1 Corinthians 6:9-13

Don't you realize that this is not the way to live? Unjust people who don't care about God will not be joining in his kingdom. Those who use and abuse each other, use and abuse sex, use and abuse the earth and everything in it, don't qualify as citizens in God's kingdom. A number of you know from experience what I'm talking about, for not so long ago you were on that list. Since then, you've been cleaned up and given a fresh start by Jesus, our Master, our Messiah, and by our God present in us, the Spirit.

Just because something is technically legal doesn't mean that it's spiritually appropriate. If I went around doing whatever I thought I could get by with, I'd be a slave to my whims.

You know the old saying, "First you eat to live, and then you live to eat"? Well, it may be true that the body is only a temporary thing, but that's no excuse for stuffing your body with food, or indulging it with sex. Since the Master honors you with a body, honor him with your body!

THINK

- What do you think prompted Paul to write about the use and abuse of sex?
- If you are one of those who was "not long ago on that list," in what respects do you feel "cleaned up and given a fresh start by Jesus"? In what respects *don't* you feel that?
- Where does what's technically legal for you become spiritually inappropriate for you? For instance, are you unable to even be in a video-rental shop if you know there's an adult section in the back? Where do you draw your line?

THINK (CONTINUED)

PRAY

Lord, help me to honor you by . . .

READ Killing Off Lust

Colossians 3:4-5

When Christ (your real life, remember) shows up again on this earth, you'll show up, too—the real you, the glorious you. Meanwhile, be content with obscurity, like Christ.

And that means killing off everything connected with that way of death: sexual promiscuity, impurity, lust, doing whatever you feel like whenever you feel like it, and grabbing whatever attracts your fancy. That's a life shaped by things and feelings instead of by God.

THINK

- How is our society shaped by a "do whatever you feel like" mentality? How does that impact your ability to "be content with obscurity"?
- In what ways are lust and promiscuity (and the rest of the above list) "connected with that way of death"? Isn't that rather extreme?
- What does it take to kill off lust? What is difficult about this?
- In what ways is your life still shaped by things and feelings instead of by God?

PRAY

God, teach me how to . . .

READ   Bedroom Eyes

Proverbs 6:20-28

> Good friend, follow your father's good advice;
>   Don't wander off from your mother's teachings.
> Wrap yourself in them from head to foot;
>   wear them like a scarf around your neck.
> Wherever you walk, they'll guide you;
>   whenever you rest, they'll guard you;
>   when you wake up, they'll tell you what's next.
> For sound advice is a beacon,
>   good teaching is a light,
>   moral discipline is a life path.
>
> They'll protect you from wanton women,
>   from the seductive talk of some temptress.
> Don't lustfully fantasize on her beauty,
>   nor be taken in by her bedroom eyes.
> You can buy an hour with a whore for a loaf of bread,
>   but a wanton woman may well eat *you* alive.
> Can you build a fire in your lap
>   and not burn your pants?
> Can you walk barefoot on hot coals
>   and not get blisters?

THINK

- What "sound advice" have you been given that should help you know how to deal with lustful thoughts?
- Why do men often ignore the wisdom of others when it comes to lustful thinking? Why is lust such a strong temptation?
- How is giving in to lust like walking "barefoot on hot coals"? Is it inevitable that lusting leads to harm?

- Think about a time you've been tempted by someone's "bedroom eyes." What led to that temptation? How might you have avoided getting into that situation?

PRAY

God, your truth challenges me to . . .

READ A Little Red Lizard

From *The Great Divorce*, by C. S. Lewis[5]

I saw coming towards us a ghost who carried something on his shoulder. Like all the Ghosts, he was unsubstantial, but they differed from one another as smokes differ. Some had been whitish; this one was dark and oily. What sat on his shoulder was a little red lizard, and it was twitching its tail like a whip and whispering things in his ear. As we caught sight of him he turned his head to the reptile with a snarl of impatience. "Shut up, I tell you!" he said. It wagged its tail and continued to whisper to him. He ceased snarling, and presently began to smile. Then he turned and started to limp westward, away from the mountains.

"Off so soon?" said a voice.

The speaker was more or less human in shape but larger than a man, and so bright that I could hardly look at him. His presence smote on my eyes and on my body, too (for there was heat coming from him as well as light) like the morning sun at the beginning of a tyrannous summer day.

"Yes. I'm off," said the Ghost. "Thanks for all your hospitality. But it's no good, you see. I told this little chap (here he indicated the Lizard) that he'd have to be quiet if he came—which he insisted on doing. Of course his stuff won't do here: I realise that. But he won't stop. I shall just have to go home."

"Would you like me to make him quiet?" said the flaming spirit—an angel, as I now understood.

"Of course I would," said the Ghost.

"Then I will kill him," said the Angel, taking a step forward.

"Oh—ah—look out! You're burning me. Keep away," said the Ghost, retreating.

"Don't you want him killed?"

"You didn't say anything about killing him at first. I hardly meant to bother you with anything so drastic as that."

"It's the only way," said the Angel, whose burning hands were now very close to the Lizard. "Shall I kill it?"

"Well, that's a further question. I'm quite open to consider it, but it's a new point, isn't it? I mean, for the moment I was only thinking about silencing it because up here—well, it's so damned embarrassing."

"May I kill it?"

"Well, there's time to discuss that later."

"There is no time. May I kill it?"

"Please, I never meant to be such a nuisance. Please—really—don't bother. Look! It's gone to sleep of its own accord. I'm sure it'll be all right now. Thanks ever so much."

"May I kill it?"

"Honestly, I don't think there's the slightest necessity for that. I'm sure I shall be able to keep it in order now. I think the gradual process would be far better than killing it."

"The gradual process is of no use at all."

"Don't you think so? Well, I'll think over what you've said very carefully. I honestly will. In fact I'd let you kill it now, but as a matter of fact I'm not feeling frightfully well today. It would be silly to do it now. I'd need to be in good health for the operation. Some other day, perhaps."

"There is no other day. All days are present now."

"Get back! You're burning me. How can I tell you to kill it? You'd kill me if you did."

"It is not so."

"Why, you're hurting me now."

"I never said it wouldn't hurt you. I said it wouldn't kill you."

"Oh, I know. You think I'm a coward. But it isn't that. Really it isn't. I say! Let me run back by tonight's bus and get an opinion from my own doctor. I'll come again the first moment I can."

THINK

- This passage has generally been interpreted as a man's battle with lust. How close is this image of lust to the kind you feel and battle?

- Has your problem with lust been solved dealt with as definitively as this man's, or have you experienced a more gradual deliverance? Or do you feel that God apparently expects you to live with it for life?
- One reason the man was reluctant to let the Angel "operate" on him was because of the anticipated pain. What pain (if any) did you experience (or are you experiencing) when you began saying no to the temptation of lust?

PRAY

Lord, give me wisdom and patience to . . .

LIVE

What I Want to Discuss

What have you discovered this week that you definitely want to discuss with your small group? Write that here. Then begin your small-group discussion with these thoughts.

So What?

Use the following space to summarize the truths you uncovered about the reality of lust in your life and what you need to do to overcome that temptation. Review your "Beginning Place" if you need to remember where you began. How does God's truth impact the "next step" in your journey?

Then What?

What is one practical thing you can do to apply what you've discovered? Describe how you would put this into practice. What steps would you take? Remember to think realistically—an admirable but unreachable goal is as good as no goal. Discuss your goal in your small group to further define it.

How?

Identify how you will be held accountable to the goal you described. Who will be on your support team? What are their responsibilities? How will you measure the success of your plan? Write the details here.

TEMPTATION TO CHEAT YOUR BOSS

"With as little as I'm getting paid around here, I ought to be able to use the company computer for personal business. And so what if I take a long lunch once in a while?"

A REMINDER:

Before you dive into this study, spend a little time reviewing what you wrote in the previous lesson's "Live" sections. How are you doing? Check with your small-group members and review your progress toward the specified goals. If necessary, adjust your goals and plans, and then recommit to them.

THE BEGINNING PLACE

The only Christian work is good work, well done.

—DOROTHY L. SAYERS

Unless you work out of your home, you'll likely spend a good chunk of time at your job site—in an office, a truck cab, or out in the field. And most of the conversations in your life will likely be work-centered.

It stands to reason that many if not most of your temptations will also beset you at work—temptations to take more than you give, to slack off now and then, to return the kick when you get kicked, perhaps even to replenish your drawers at home with office supplies from work.

As you might expect, the Bible is packed with anecdotes, advice, and mandates covering this subject. Genesis chapters 29 and 30 relate the shrewd connivance that Jacob used to cheat Laban, his father-in-law and employer, out of the best livestock. (Then again, Laban had earlier cheated Jacob, so did he deserve it? The Pentateuch's writer implies as much.)

The Proverbs are known to commend shrewdness, too, as well as hard work and honesty. And Jesus told his followers to "be as cunning as a snake, inoffensive as a dove" (Matthew 10:16). Okay, there's nothing here to suggest that we should *cheat* our boss, but "cunning as a snake" certainly seems to hint at a little necessary hardball now and then, doesn't it? And the apostle Paul's commands—well, you'll read some of them later in this lesson. He not only expects you to never give less than 110 percent to your boss but also to serve him or her as if you're working for God himself!

So where does this all leave you at work when you're tempted? Do you use company equipment for personal business? Is arriving fifteen minutes late to work most days and leaving promptly at five cheating your boss? Is *not* notifying your boss when you see outright wrong stuff going down indirectly cheating your company? Unless you're one of those types that leap out of bed every morning with a smile on your face and a "What good can I do for my boss today?" on your lips, you're probably tempted to shortchange him or her somehow and pocket the change.

In the face of such temptations, what does "good work, well done" look like—at your job, in your office, with your coworkers?

Use the space below to summarize your beginning place for this lesson. Describe your realities as well as your desires about the temptations you feel to give your company or your boss less than your best—or even to cheat them. We'll start here and then go deeper.

READ Stealing Office Supplies

From the *Tampa Tribune* article "An Inside Job," by Dave Simanoff[1]

Most people don't start out at a company with the intent of ripping it off. Some 70 percent of people involved in occupational fraud and abuse had never been charged or convicted with a crime before, according to the fraud examiners' survey.

Paul Spector, a professor of industrial organizational psychology at the University of South Florida, said workers are most likely to lash out against an employer when they are stressed, dissatisfied or don't feel empowered.

"If employees don't feel they have control, and they're stressed or upset, that's a formula for misbehavior," he said. Sometimes workers feel entitled to steal because they think they have been mistreated.

"If you feel like you've been ripped off by the company, then you're going to rip off the company," he said.

Scott Adams, the cartoonist who chronicles cubicle life in "Dilbert," says workers today feel upset because they are being forced to do more work and because they can't easily switch jobs because the economy is poor.

"People are always disgruntled when they think they don't have options," he said. "If it feels like things are going wrong in your office, you can't leave, so it's probably your boss's fault. He must pay in sticky notes and expense accounts and sick days."

One of Adams' first Dilbert books was *Build a Better Life by Stealing Office Supplies.*

"In a very small way, [stealing office supplies] can make you feel better," Adams said. "It can make you feel like you did something to get even."

That might not seem fair, "but the beauty of the concept of fairness is that it's so flexible," he said. "It can mean what you want it to mean."

Proverbs 27:18

> If you care for your orchard, you'll enjoy its fruit;
>> if you honor your boss, you'll be honored.

THINK

- Is office theft a problem in your workplace? When have you been tempted to take office supplies home?
- How might stealing office supplies make you "feel better"? What are better options for dealing with perceived unfairness?
- In what ways is your boss like your orchard? (Imagine yourself a peach or apple or hazelnut grower for a minute.)
- How fail-safe do you feel this Proverbs promise is—that if you honor your boss, you'll be honored? Do you have any experience that supports this claim? Any experience that contradicts this claim?

PRAY

God, help me to honor . . .

READ Misconduct in the Workplace

From the executive summary of the 2003 National Business Ethics Survey, by the Ethics Resource Center[2]

Findings from a survey conducted among U.S. employees by the Washington-based Ethics Resource Center:

- Nearly a third of respondents say their coworkers condone questionable ethics practices by showing respect for those who achieve success using them.
- The types of misconduct most frequently observed in 2003 include: abusive or intimidating behavior (21%); misreporting of hours worked (20%); lying (19%); and withholding needed information (18%).
- Employees in transitioning organizations (undergoing mergers, acquisitions or restructurings) observe misconduct and feel pressure at rates that are nearly double those in more stable organizations.
- Compared with other employees, younger managers (under age 30) with low tenure in their organizations (less than 3 years) are twice as likely to feel pressure to compromise ethics standards (21% versus 10%).
- Despite an overall increase in reporting of misconduct, nearly half of all non-management employees (44%) still do not report the misconduct they observe. The top two reasons given for not reporting misconduct are: (1) a belief that no corrective action will be taken and (2) fear that the report will not be kept confidential.
- Younger employees with low tenure are among the least likely to report misconduct (43% as compared with 69% for all other employees). They are also among the most likely to feel that management and coworkers will view them negatively if they report.
- Less than three in five employees (58%) who report misconduct are satisfied with the response of their organizations.

- In many areas, views of ethics remain "rosier at the top." For example, senior and middle managers have less fear of reporting misconduct and are more satisfied with the response of their organizations. They also feel that honesty and respect are practiced more frequently than do lower level employees.

THINK

- Which of these findings best reflect what you've observed over the years in your places of employment? Which best reflect what you've personally experienced?
- Has your job security ever been threatened by something unethical that you saw or heard? How was the situation resolved? What change if any did it make in you?
- Do you feel that management actually knows what is going on in your office and the offices of peers? Why or why not?
- If you're in management, do *you* know what's going on? Is ignorance of unethical behavior akin to condoning theft in your company? Explain.

PRAY

Father, help me to speak up when . . .

READ   Servant = Employee?

Ephesians 6:5-8

Servants, respectfully obey your earthly masters but always with
an eye to obeying the real master, Christ. Don't just do what you
have to do to get by, but work heartily, as Christ's servants doing
what God wants you to do. And work with a smile on your face,
always keeping in mind that no matter who happens to be giving the orders, you're really serving God. Good work will get
you good pay from the Master, regardless of whether you are
slave or free.

Colossians 3:22-25

Servants, do what you're told by your earthly masters. And don't
just do the minimum that will get you by. Do your best. Work
from the heart for your real Master, for God, confident that you'll
get paid in full when you come into your inheritance. Keep in
mind always that the ultimate Master you're serving is Christ. The
sullen servant who does shoddy work will be held responsible.
Being Christian doesn't cover up bad work.

THINK

- In what ways does the apostle's mandate strike you as almost
  maniacally cheery?
- From your experience, how realistic are these commands?
- Have you ever been in a job—or are you in one now—in
  which your coworkers actually dissuade you when you try to
  "work heartily" and not "just do what you have to do to get
  by"? What are your options in such a situation?
- Such difficulties aside for the moment, what one or two things
  that Paul says here *could* you actually do? If you can't fulfill
  the whole shebang, where can you inch forward a little toward
  the ideal?

- Have you ever actually tried to picture Jesus as your *real* boss and work accordingly? What was it like?

PRAY

Lord, you know how difficult it is for me to . . .

READ   Honesty Versus Competence

From the *Nation's Business* article "Leading By Example May Promote Worker Honesty," by Roberta Maynard[3]

> "At one time I hired people with dental talents," says Dr. Jim Cuglewski of Parma, Ohio, a dentist and president of his 13-year-old practice Cuglewski, Timko & Associates. "About five years ago, I started hiring people who knew right from wrong." He has developed a set of interview questions to gauge how someone would react in certain situations, and references are always asked outright whether the candidate is honest.

THINK

- Ever known a boss to seemingly care more about her employees' honesty than about their competence? What was it like to work in that atmosphere?
- How do companies like Enron figure into the equation—when the boss is looking out only for himself and will advance the company's interests at any cost, regardless of ethics?
- The good doctor Cuglewski apparently believes that it is easier to teach someone dental skills than it is to teach them honesty. To what extent do you agree?

PRAY

God, show me the way to . . .

READ A Web of Temptation

From the *Database and Network Journal* article "The Temptations of the Web," by Paul Sloane[4]

There are few modern businesses that could survive without the Web: an indispensable source of information on any subject, and the most rapid and effective form of correspondence. Unfortunately, Internet connectivity also creates a host of temptations. According to a recent survey carried out by corporate Internet access management company SurfControl, up to 60 percent of employees' Internet activity includes visits to unproductive, inappropriate, and potentially dangerous sites.

So what, you may say, *if employees break up their day with a bit of personal surfing on the Web. Nobody can be expected to work consistently without an occasional break.* But as the Internet and all things e-related gradually take over the workplace, the problem is getting more serious. A little personal shopping during a lunch break can cause permanent damage to an employer in terms of productivity loss, bandwidth loss, and legal liability.

On average, non-work-related surfing costs U.S. businesses $54 billion and 30 – 40 percent in productivity losses every year. According to the Gartner Group, businesses lose an estimated 26 million man hours annually to online game playing alone. One unnamed U.S. government department, for example, discovered an elaborate ring of computer blackjack gamblers operating in its offices—gaming that cost the department thousands of dollars not only in downtime hours, but also in expensive solutions to curb the problem.

Other popular at-work surfing activities include sending emails to friends and family, visiting news groups, checking sports scores, and searching for other jobs. All of which wreak havoc on a company's bandwidth. Last year nearly two million people logged on to a 25-minute Victoria's Secret fashion show Webcast during business hours, using a bandwidth capacity equivalent to nearly 200 million T1 lines.

THINK

- Is it realistic to abstain from personal business on your company computer? To not make personal calls on your business phone? At what point does a professional "separation of powers" become silly or even counterproductive?
- In what ways might personal use of the company Internet shortchange your employer?
- If your firm has a policy that forbids personal use of company computers, do you honor the *intent* of the policy as well as the specifics? Or do you use your computer for personal tasks you feel are reasonable? Do you think God allows you this kind of wiggle room?
- If personal computer use isn't a big deal in your work, why isn't it? What use of your computer *would* be cheating your company?

PRAY

God, help me to be consistent with . . .

READ The Big Boss and the Bottom Line

Isaiah 58:3-6

> "'Why do we fast and you don't look our way?
> Why do we humble ourselves and you don't even notice?'"
>
> "Well, here's why:
>
> "The bottom line on your 'fast days' is profit.
> You drive your employees much too hard. . . .
> You fast, but you swing a mean fist.
> The kind of fasting you do
> won't get your prayers off the ground.
> Do you think this is the kind of fast day I'm after:
> a day to show off humility?
> To put on a pious long face
> and parade around solemnly in black?
> Do you call *that* fasting,
> a fast day that I, GOD, would like?
>
> "This is the kind of fast day I'm after:
> to break the chains of injustice,
> get rid of exploitation in the workplace,
> free the oppressed,
> cancel debts."

THINK

- Think about temptations on the *other* side of the desk—temptations in the twentieth floor's corner office. Think Enron and Tyco. What does God say about this, through that prophetic mouthpiece of his named Isaiah?
- How in this economic climate can owners *not* be draconian in staying competitive? How can a Christian CEO obey God and yet maintain a thriving business?

- Is it more permissible in our society for corporate executives to cheat their employees than for employees to cheat their corporations? For whom is the temptation greatest? How do the results of both kinds of cheating compare? What are the consequences if either is caught?

PRAY

Father, give me the strength and courage to . . .

READ In Small Things

Luke 16:10-12

> If you're honest in small things,
>   you'll be honest in big things;
> If you're a crook in small things,
>   you'll be a crook in big things.
> If you're not honest in small jobs,
>   who will put you in charge of the store?

THINK

- What "small things" are you tempted to be dishonest about at work? How are the "small things" any different from the "big things"?
- Is it true that people who are dishonest in small things will also be dishonest in big things? Explain.
- What part does your personal workplace integrity play into your chances for promotion at work? Does having honesty and integrity at work always equate to better promotion chances? Why or why not?

PRAY

God, help me live with integrity by . . .

LIVE

What I Want to Discuss

What have you discovered this week that you definitely want to discuss with your small group? Write that here. Then begin your small-group discussion with these thoughts.

So What?

Use the following space to summarize the truths you uncovered about cheating in the workplace and what it might take to overcome that temptation. Review your "Beginning Place" if you need to remember where you began. How does God's truth impact the "next step" in your journey?

Then What?

What is one practical thing you can do to apply what you've discovered? Describe how you would put this into practice. What steps would you take? Remember to think realistically—an admirable but unreachable goal is as good as no goal. Discuss your goal in your small group to further define it.

How?

Identify how you will be held accountable to the goal you described. Who will be on your support team? What are their responsibilities? How will you measure the success of your plan? Write the details here.

TEMPTATION TO ENGAGE IN AN AFFAIR

"She's a good friend—that's all. Can't men have close friendships with women who aren't their wives?"

A REMINDER:

Before you dive into this study, spend a little time reviewing what you wrote in the previous lesson's "Live" sections. How are you doing? Check with your small-group members and review your progress toward the specified goals. If necessary, adjust your goals and plans, and then recommit to them.

> **A note to unmarried men:** This lesson isn't just for married men. Perhaps you're dating someone, whether seriously or casually. How do you deal with the temptation to invest emotionally or sexually in a woman when you have no particular intention to marry her? The temptation to "stray" is just as strong for you as for someone who has spoken marriage vows. We're not suggesting that casual dating is the same as a long-term commitment. That's not the point. The point is, no matter what relationships you're in (even friendships), the temptation to replace what you already have with "something new" is strong. That's mostly true about sexual desires, but it also is true about emotional needs as well (and, yes, we men do have emotional needs).

THE BEGINNING PLACE

Looked at from one perspective, lifelong monogamy seems an unlikely proposition. Even a lifelong monogamist will tell you that over the course of his life he becomes a different person. Sure, a lot about us never changes, but at the same time, everything changes.

So why not mates? Is God's clear law against anything but absolute celibacy or absolute monogamy our only defense against what some think is fundamental male wiring to preserve their DNA through mating with as many women as possible? (Sort of like diversifying your mutual-funds portfolio as a hedge against one or another of them drying up.) If this is so, how many years can a man realistically maintain his resolve to obey God in the face of such odds? Where is a spiritual Viagra when you need it, to keep up your determination to do the right thing?

Let's scale things back a bit. You say you have no desire to sleep your way through the women in your office. You are married—"happily married" may be how you put it. Are there relational lines you should not cross? For example, is it appropriate to go out to lunch with a male colleague but not a female one? Is it okay to go out with a female colleague just once? Regularly? What if she's a good friend as well as a colleague? Do different men have different thresholds for being able to separate romance from an intimate, nonsexual friendship with a woman not his wife? How about you—do you recognize when a friendship floats toward romance? How do you respond? Or does God require (or suggest) that when you marry, you forfeit not only sex with other women but close friendship, too?

Use the space below to summarize your beginning place for this lesson. Describe your realities as well as your desires about emotionally and sexually investing in women you're not married to. We'll start here and then go deeper.

READ Fighting the Ache

From "Ben" in *Between Sundays*, by Douglas Young[1]

He'd not quarreled with his wife: indeed, he loved and respected and cared for Margery. It was this other girl who filled his thoughts day and night. He could not, he said, live without her. And had decided that he would not try to do so.

"Does she work in your firm?" I asked when he came to see me, his minister.

"She is my secretary."

Oh dear! It was all so usual, so trite, so obvious. The same old story. The passing affair with a pretty, young girl. I groaned inwardly. Who would have thought Ben capable of anything so trivial?

They came to my house together on the following Wednesday. I was surprised. There was nothing trivial about her. She had a soft expression, kind eyes. Troubled eyes. Both she and Ben said responsible, sensible things. It seemed that they had had no physical relationship; only, so far, a magnetic, urgently compelling rapport. They were deeply satisfied together and profoundly miserable apart.

Here, I realized, was nothing so ordinary as a passing infatuation.

On the occasion of their last visit with me, they looked tired and unhappy. They'd decided, they said. She would take a job with a different firm in a distant town. He was to return to his family.

Margery, with whom I'd been in constant touch, took the news with mixed feelings.

The effect upon Ben was dramatic. When, after six months, his health continued to deteriorate, Margery became alarmed: her love outweighed her resentment. At her suggestion, I spoke with him.

"Talk about it, Ben," I said. "It often helps."

Ben dragged it out of himself. "I didn't intend it to be so. I was never one for a passing affair. Wasn't looking for one then. It just came to me one day that, with life so short, it couldn't be wrong to send over a signal of appreciation to one who had

become so special to me. It was all very honourable and propri-
etous. Even sober." He gestured. "The younger generation would
think it square."

"So if it was a mistake, Ben, it was one of inexperience?
Anyway, you think you did the right thing in coming home?"

"Yes," flatly. "A man's place is in his home, looking after his
wife and children."

"So at least you've got that satisfaction?"

"Yes. But I've also got this ache. A physical ache—like
homesickness—eating me away inside."

Margery and Ben stayed together. Margery recovered first. Ben
was never quite the same again. His was the problem of a man
stressed by the possession of both extra honor and extra love.

Some loves are not permissible, not legitimate to express.
But—they can be real.

THINK

- How close to Ben's experience have you come at one point or
  another in your life?
- To what degree do you agree or disagree with Ben's minister
  that some loves, although impermissible, can be authentic?
- Why do you suppose Ben decided to stay with Margery instead
  of start over with his secretary? Were these good reasons?
- What would you say to Ben about the physical ache ("like homesickness") he claims to have? Would you advise him to get over it?

PRAY

Lord, I confess that I . . .

READ Leering Looks

Matthew 5:27-29

You know the next commandment pretty well, too: "Don't go to bed with another's spouse." But don't think you've preserved your virtue simply by staying out of bed. Your heart can be corrupted by lust even quicker than your body. Those leering looks you think nobody notices—they also corrupt.

Let's not pretend this is easier than it really is. If you want to live a morally pure life, here's what you have to do: You have to blind your right eye the moment you catch it in a lustful leer. You have to choose to live one-eyed or else be dumped on a moral trash pile.

THINK

- Jesus makes this issue sound cut-and-dried: Either excise what makes you sin, or "be dumped on a moral trash pile." Have you spent any time in your life on such a pile? What did that feel like?
- Jesus' point was that you've got to make some hard decisions if you want to avoid sinning—especially if you're inclined to a given sort of sin. Perhaps you're like many men—at the very least, tempted to *imagine* sleeping with a woman you're not married to. What sacrifice must you consider making if you want to avoid leering and lusting?
- Do you think Jesus knew sexual temptation? Explain. What implications does your answer have for how you deal with sexual temptation?
- In what circumstances are you most susceptible to *mentally* or *imaginatively* going to bed with a woman you're not married to? Where does it get really tough for you?

THINK (CONTINUED)

PRAY

God, I need your help to . . .

READ More Than Skin on Skin

From *The Screwtape Letters*, by C. S. Lewis[2]

The truth is that wherever a man lies with a woman, there, whether they like it or not, a transcendental relation is set up between them which must be eternally enjoyed or eternally endured. From the true statement that this transcendental relation was intended to produce, and, if obediently entered into, too often *will* produce, affection and the family, humans can be made to infer the false belief that the blend of affection, fear, and desire which they call "being in love" is the only thing that makes marriage either happy or holy.

1 Corinthians 6:16-20

Remember that your bodies are created with the same dignity as the Master's body. You wouldn't take the Master's body off to a whorehouse, would you? I should hope not.

There's more to sex than mere skin on skin. Sex is as much spiritual mystery as physical fact. As written in Scripture, "The two become one." Since we want to become spiritually one with the Master, we must not pursue the kind of sex that avoids com-mitment and intimacy, leaving us more lonely than ever—the kind of sex that can never "become one." There is a sense in which sexual sins are different from all others. In sexual sin we violate the sacredness of our own bodies, these bodies that were made for God-given and God-modeled love, for "becoming one" with another. Or didn't you realize that your body is a sacred place, the place of the Holy Spirit? Don't you see that you can't live however you please, squandering what God paid such a high price for? The physical part of you is not some piece of property belonging to the spiritual part of you. God owns the whole works. So let people see God in and through your body.

THINK

- Respond to Lewis's comment that sexual connectedness—even a one-night stand—must be "eternally enjoyed or eternally endured."
- Do you believe it is accurate to say that the animal pleasure of skin on skin is God's gift to us just as sexuality's sacred mystery is a gift? Why or why not?
- What movie, novel, or story have you seen or read that acknowledges this sacred and mysterious aspect of sex? Was the mysterious connectedness enjoyed or endured?
- What was Paul getting at when he said that "in sexual sin we violate the sacredness of our own bodies"?
- If not falling in love, then what *is* it that makes marriage happy or holy? Is romance necessary, after all? Think about this.

PRAY

Lord, help me to appreciate . . .

READ It Started Innocently

From *The Sun* feature "Readers Write"[3]

Last year I fell in lust with a programmer at work. We do the strange dance of attraction around each other. In another life, we might have been two beatniks speeding down Route 66 in a convertible, theorizing about the meaning of life. He is married and, like me, would never leave his spouse for fear of losing his kids.

It started when we innocently went to lunch one day—to [complain] about work, as we often do—and on the way back to the car, he grabbed me, swung me around, and kissed me in the rain. To my surprise, I kissed back. My façade [of being happily and wonderfully satisfied in my marriage] burned to the ground.

We have never consummated our relationship (if you call it that). Oddly, this does not bother me. I find that I can tell this man anything: my pain, my desires, my fantasies. I have never had such a truthful connection with another human being, and I value this over sex, food, and all other basic needs. He does not judge me for my opinions and emotions; he encourages me to unleash them. In this life of lies that I have created, this affair is the most honest relationship I have.

THINK

- If you could ask this woman one question, what would it be?
- Is this woman at fault for finding a connection in a man other than her husband? Explain.
- How would you weigh the comparative graces and perils of such a relationship as the writer describes?
- Talk about that one kiss in the rain. What did the kiss mean to the writer? What *didn't* it mean to her? Describe if you can a similar impulse that you once felt (or often feel) and what you did or didn't do about it.

- Though she did not sleep with her colleague, did she cross some sort of line into infidelity—of soul if not of body? Explain.

PRAY

God, give me the confidence to . . .

READ Meeting Needs

From *Sexual Arrangements*, by Janet Reibstein and Martin Richards[4]

Laura never stopped respecting her husband, who continued to be a good provider, a sensible and loyal, if distant, husband and father, and a decent, reliable, and good man. Laura had made a clear assessment of her marriage by the time she began to have affairs. Over the years her own requirements for "everything" in the marriage realm had changed. She needed more now than she had needed in the early years, but she concluded that her husband was not the one to fulfill these new needs. He was good at other things. Intimacy was not their strong suit together. Others could step in to fill the breach.

This is one way of resolving the tensions—change your expectations of marriage.

Luke 16:18

"Using the legalities of divorce
    as a cover for lust is adultery;
Using the legalities of marriage
    as a cover for lust is adultery."

THINK

- What expectations did you have of marriage when you first entered into it? (Or if you're unmarried, what expectations do you have now?)
- In what ways might you depend on your wife too much or expect her to fulfill too many of your needs or expectations? Where in the Bible can you find evidence that a wife should fulfill all of her husband's expectations—as friend, lover, companion, financial partner, parenting partner?
- Is our culture hung up on the idea that it is our inalienable right to have our needs met? How does this impact your marriage relationship?

- What do you think Jesus meant by "using the legalities of marriage as a cover for lust"? In what ways can a man use his marriage to camouflage lust? How is this adultery, according to Jesus?

PRAY

Father, point me toward . . .

READ Can We Be Friends?

From the *Psychology Today* article "Overcoming Sex," by Camille Chatterjee[5]

Society has long singled out romance as the prototypical male-female relationship because it spawns babies and keeps the life cycle going; cross-sex friendship, as researchers call it, has been either ignored or trivialized. We have rules for how to act in romantic relationships (flirt, date, get married, have kids) and even same-sex friendships (boys relate by doing activities together, girls by talking and sharing). But there are so few platonic male-female friendships on display in our culture that we're at a loss to even define these relationships.

Part of this confusion stems from the media. A certain 1989 film starring Meg Ryan and Billy Crystal convinced a nation of moviegoers that sex always comes between men and women, making true friendship impossible.

"*When Harry Met Sally* set back the potential for male-female friendship about 25 years," says Michael Monsour, Ph.D., assistant professor of communications at the University of Colorado at Denver, and author of *Women and Men as Friends: Relationships across the Life Span in the 21st Century* (Lawrence Erlbaum, 2001). Television hasn't helped either. "Almost every time you see a male-female friendship, it winds up turning into romance," Monsour notes. Think Sam and Diane or Chandler and Monica. These cultural images are hard to overcome, he says. It's no wonder we expect that men and women are always on the road to romance. . . .

A survey of more than 1,450 members of the dating website match.com revealed the following:

- Do you believe men and women can be platonic friends?
  Yes: 83%
  No: 11%
  Unsure: 6%

- Have you had a platonic friendship that crossed the line and became romantic or sexual?

  Yes: 62%

  No: 36%

  Unsure: 2%

- Who is more likely to misinterpret the intimacy of friendship for sexual desire?

  Men: 64%

  Women: 25%

  Unsure: 11%

THINK

- How would you respond to these survey questions?
- What do the apparent statistical odds against a platonic relationship staying that way say to you? Do you risk having a friendship with a woman at the office, at the lunch counter, in the dog park, at church? Describe how you have dealt with this in the past and how you intend to deal with it.
- If you know of a close friendship between a man and a woman that is a model of a friendship that has *not* flowed to romance, describe it.
- Considering the odds, why risk adultery by cultivating a close friendship with a woman not your wife? Should the walk-as-far-from-the-cliff-edge-as-possible principle apply here? Why or why not?

PRAY

God, teach me what to do when . . .

READ Eloquent Talk

Romans 2:19-23

I have a special word of caution for you who are sure that you have it all together yourselves and, because you know God's revealed Word inside and out, feel qualified to guide others through their blind alleys and dark nights and confused emotions to God. While you are guiding others, who is going to guide you? I'm quite serious. While preaching "Don't steal!" are you going to rob people blind? Who would suspect you? The same with adultery. The same with idolatry. You can get by with almost anything if you front it with eloquent talk about God and his law.

THINK

- If you were to have an affair, what excuses would you offer to rationalize the affair? What would ring most hollow about these excuses?
- What do you believe drives most men to have affairs?
- Respond to this quote: "Infidelity isn't about whom you lie with. It's whom you lie to."
- What lies do men tell themselves in order to defend their decision to have affairs? How are those lies examples of the "eloquent talk" described in Romans?

PRAY

God, direct me to the truth about . . .

LIVE

What I Want to Discuss

What have you discovered this week that you definitely want to discuss
with your small group? Write that here. Then begin your small-group
discussion with these thoughts.

So What?

Use the following space to summarize the truths you uncovered about
the temptation to have an affair and how to overcome it. Review your
"Beginning Place" if you need to remember where you began. How
does God's truth impact the "next step" in your journey?

Then What?

What is one practical thing you can do to apply what you've discovered?
Describe how you would put this into practice. What steps would you
take? Remember to think realistically—an admirable but unreachable
goal is as good as no goal. Discuss your goal in your small group to
further define it.

How?

Identify how you will be held accountable to the goal you described.
Who will be on your support team? What are their responsibilities? How
will you measure the success of your plan? Write the details here.

TEMPTATION TO GIVE UP ON FATHERING

"Around the time my daughter turned thirteen, for the
first time she shut her bedroom door—and shut me out.
So now I venture into her life only when invited."

A REMINDER:

*Before you dive into this study, spend a little time reviewing what
you wrote in the previous lesson's "Live" sections. How are you
doing? Check with your small-group members and review your
progress toward the specified goals. If necessary, adjust your goals
and plans, and then recommit to them.*

THE BEGINNING PLACE

You are encouraged by your parents, teachers, professors, bosses, pastors, and the media to strive for greatness, to score highly, to make something of yourself. Those who do, however— *really* do—always pay a price for what they achieve. And often the price is a domestic one—a parental one. Men especially, it seems, don't multitask well

> **A note to men without children:** Yes, this lesson is specifically written to men who have sons and daughters, but no, you shouldn't skip this lesson if you don't have a family. You see, this lesson is really all about avoiding the temptation to abdicate responsibility. While we explore that temptation in the context of parenting, much of what you'll read here applies to other areas of life. Look here for truths that can apply to your unique circumstances.

emotionally when the career ladder needs climbing, or even when a humble job needs attention. (And what job these days *doesn't* need a lot of attention if you're to hang on to it?)

You've no doubt heard the stories about men (and women, too) who eschew or sacrifice political or corporate status for their families' sakes, for the good of their children, in order to maintain or restore the home front. Yet how credible are such anecdotes? Can you afford not to focus primarily on your job? Is there a trick to connecting meaningfully with your family while still excelling at your work? Where exactly are you tempted to abdicate responsibility? How are you coping with, dealing with, rationalizing, or otherwise enduring such temptation?

Use the space below to summarize your beginning place for this lesson. Describe your realities as well as your desires about your family and temptations to withdraw from them. We'll start here and then go deeper.

READ   The Evolving Family

From *Life Without Father*, by David Popenoe[1]

Families have evolved considerably since Victorian times. According to author David Popenoe, here are some of the more significant changes:

- Increased reliance on romantic love
- Decreased interest in social obligation
- Greater focus on self-fulfillment
- The decline of a religious connection
- The shrinking role of fathers in day-to-day family activities
- The movement of married women into the labor force

THINK

- Where do you see these processes at work in society?
- How, if at all, have these processes influenced you, your expectations, your relationships, and your job or career?
- How do highly specialized jobs pull husbands and fathers out of day-to-day family activities?

PRAY

Father, help me to make decisions that . . .

READ   The Abandoned Child

From the *Mothering* editorial "Who's in Charge?" by Peggy O'Mara [2]

I hear parents say that their teens need privacy, want to be alone, and that mothers and fathers are afraid to trespass. Parents can interpret the surly, silent behavior of their teens as a personal rejection and abdicate their parental authority in the face of this onslaught, or they can interpret this behavior as a cry for help. Curiously, those teens who seem so independent, only because they are so distant, are often the ones who get into trouble. The honors student with numerous extracurricular activities is the one who surprises us with a drug or alcohol problem. Parents seeking help from our local parents' assistance center are not the poor, minority families, but rather the white, professional families whose children are modeling their parents' overcommitted lifestyles.

Because the decisions that my teens are now making— regarding driving, sex, drugs, and their futures—could be life- and-death decisions, more than ever, they need my counsel. They do not need me to control them, but neither do they need me to relinquish them to the world. I sneak in mini-lectures in the car, in the kitchen, and around the house. I am confident that I have wisdom to share, but most often, I simply share my own experiences. And I am careful not to take responsibility for my teens' actions or behavior.

I believe that a child whose parents abdicate their authority when challenged feels abandoned. It is the abandoned child who is wounded and who must act out as a rebel, a conformist, or a victim. This acting out creates clear boundaries within which to become an adult. When we assume that the teen who is surly and crabby wants to go it alone and does not need help, we give him or her a false sense of security and the message that problem solving is a solitary endeavor—that the adult solves problems alone. Our job as parents is to move our children from dependence to independence, but this movement occurs in fits and bursts, not in linear fashion or according to a timetable. Character and maturity develop, but they are not guaranteed by age. Only experience in self-regulation teaches self-regulation.

My children respond differently to me when I have confidence in my own authority than when I do not. I no longer accept arguments on matters of helping one another, sharing chores around the house, or disrespectful and unkind behavior. And I insist that my teens communicate with me so that they do not take out school experiences on those of us at home. Peace in my home is not negotiable.

The teen years are a bridge from childhood to adulthood—a passage, a transfer of power. The teen walks the bridge, makes mistakes, plunges, holds back. The parents are the bumper rails along the sides of the bridge. The parents are available to bounce off of, but they do not do the walking. I can insist that my children respect my authority and my personal limitations because I have no ambivalence about my love, respect, and devotion to them.

As children challenge your authority, test your ways, and question your lifestyle, keep in touch. Don't let them go it alone too soon. Don't be intimidated into giving up the authority that your position in the family requires. If you don't claim your authority, someone else in the family will. And even if you are not wise, or do not feel wise, remember that your authority is not based on being right. It is based on who you are. You are the parent. You are the one in charge. That's the way it's supposed to be.

THINK

- Do you believe "surly, silent" teenage angst has always characterized the transition from child to adult, or that it is a product of our particular culture? Explain.
- How do you keep in touch with your kids as they "challenge your authority, test your ways, and question your lifestyle"?
- Respond to O'Mara's claim that a child whose parents abdicate their authority when challenged feels abandoned.

- "Your authority is not based on being right," O'Mara writes. "It is based on who you are." To what extent do you agree or disagree? Why?
- What resources do you need to help you endure this season of parenting? Where would you find such resources?

PRAY

Lord, give me the words to say when . . .

READ   Rethinking Abuse

From the *Rocky Mountain News* article "Coach's 'Abuse' of Wife Spawned Promise Keepers," by Jean Torkelson[3]

> To understand Promise Keepers, one first has to understand who its founder is: an absentee father who ignored his wife and kids while racking up football wins for the University of Colorado.
>
> "In those years, my wife was abused," wrote Bill McCartney. "Not the physical kind of abuse, but the kind that's insidious. . . . I simply did not take the time to be the husband and father I could and should have been."

1 Timothy 3:12-13

> Servants in the church are to be committed to their spouses, attentive to their own children, and diligent in looking after their own affairs. Those who do this servant work will come to be highly respected, a real credit to this Jesus-faith.

THINK

- What is your reaction to the premise that an absentee father is an abusive father?
- What, if anything, can you say from experience about being a good family provider at the expense of being an involved father or husband?
- Is the emotional abandonment of family inevitable for men who seek (and find) success in the workplace? How can you avoid this while still being a good provider for your family?
- What might it look like to live out the truth of this 1 Timothy passage in your own family? Is "high respect" the goal or the result of being committed to your family? Explain.

THINK (CONTINUED)

PRAY

God, I admit that I sometimes . . .

READ The Sons of David

From 2 Samuel 13 (Amnon's story)

Some time later, this happened: Absalom, David's son, had a sister who was very attractive. Her name was Tamar. Amnon, also David's son, was in love with her. Amnon was obsessed with his sister Tamar to the point of making himself sick over her. She was a virgin, so he couldn't see how he could get his hands on her.

Then he said to Tamar, "Bring the food into my bedroom, where we can eat in privacy." She took the nourishing dumplings she had prepared and brought them to her brother Amnon in his bedroom. But when she got ready to feed him, he grabbed her and said, "Come to bed with me, sister!"

"No, brother!" she said, "Don't hurt me! This kind of thing isn't done in Israel! Don't do this terrible thing! Where could I ever show my face? And you—you'll be out on the street in disgrace. Oh, please! Speak to the king—he'll let you marry me."

But he wouldn't listen. Being much stronger than she, he raped her.

From 2 Samuel 13-15; 18 (Absalom's story)

When Absalom fled, he went to Talmai son of Ammihud, king of Geshur. He was there three years. The king finally gave up trying to get back at Absalom. He had come to terms with Amnon's death.

[Five years later] Absalom was then summoned—he came and bowed deeply in reverence before his father David. And the king kissed Absalom.

Whenever someone would treat him with special honor, he'd shrug it off and treat him like an equal, making him feel important. Absalom did this to everyone who came to do business with the king and stole the hearts of everyone in Israel.

The conspiracy grew powerful and Absalom's supporters multiplied.

Someone came to David with the report, "The whole country has taken up with Absalom!"

"Up and out of here!" called David to all his servants who were with him in Jerusalem. "We've got to run for our lives or none of us will escape Absalom! Hurry, he's about to pull the city down around our ears and slaughter us all!"

So the king and his entire household escaped on foot.

David organized his forces. He appointed captains of thousands and captains of hundreds. Then David deployed his troops.

Absalom ran into David's men, but was out in front of them riding his mule, when the mule ran under the branches of a huge oak tree. Absalom's head was caught in the oak and he was left dangling between heaven and earth, the mule running right out from under him. A solitary soldier saw him and reported it to Joab, "I just saw Absalom hanging from an oak tree!"

Joab said to the man who told him, "If you saw him, why didn't you kill him then and there? I'd have rewarded you with ten pieces of silver and a fancy belt."

The man told Joab, "Even if I'd had a chance at a thousand pieces of silver, I wouldn't have laid a hand on the king's son. We all heard the king command you, 'For my sake, protect the young man Absalom.'"

Joab said, "I can't waste my time with you." He then grabbed three knives and stabbed Absalom in the heart while he was still alive in the tree; by then Absalom was surrounded by ten of Joab's armor bearers; they hacked away at him and killed him.

The king was stunned. Heartbroken, he went up to the room over the gate and wept. As he wept he cried out,

O my son Absalom, my dear, dear son Absalom!
Why not me rather than you, my death and not yours,
O Absalom, my dear, dear son!

From 1 Kings 1 (Adonijah's story)

King David grew old. The years had caught up with him. At this time his son Adonijah, whose mother was Haggith, puffed himself up saying, "I'm the next king!" He made quite a splash, with chariots and riders and fifty men to run ahead of him. His father had spoiled him rotten as a child, never once reprimanding him. Besides that, he was very good-looking and the next in line after Absalom.

Next Adonijah held a coronation feast, sacrificing sheep, cattle, and grain-fed heifers at the Stone of Zoheleth near the Rogel Spring. He invited all his brothers, the king's sons, and everyone in Judah who had position and influence.

Bathsheba went at once to the king in his palace bedroom. He was so old! Abishag was at his side making him comfortable. As Bathsheba bowed low, honoring the king, he said, "What do you want?"

"My master," she said, "you promised me in GOD's name, 'Your son Solomon will be king after me and sit on my throne.' And now look what's happened—Adonijah has taken over as king, and my master the king doesn't even know it!"

Then [David] ordered, "Gather my servants, then mount my son Solomon on my royal mule and lead him in procession down to Gihon. When you get there, Zadok the priest and Nathan the prophet will anoint him king over Israel. Then blow the ram's horn trumpet and shout, 'Long live King Solomon!' You will then accompany him as he enters and takes his place on my throne, succeeding me as king. I have named him ruler over Israel and Judah."

Adonijah and his retinue of guests were just finishing their "coronation" feast when they heard [the fanfare of Solomon's coronation]. "What's going on here? What's all this uproar?"

[A messenger] answered, "Our master King David has just made Solomon king!"

Panicked, Adonijah's guests got out of there, scattering every which way. But Adonijah himself, afraid for his life because of Solomon, fled to the sanctuary and grabbed the horns of the Altar.

Solomon was told, "Adonijah, fearful of King Solomon, has taken sanctuary and seized the horns of the Altar and is saying, 'I'm not leaving until King Solomon promises that he won't kill me.'"

Solomon then said, "If he proves to be a man of honor, not a hair of his head will be hurt; but if there is evil in him, he'll die." Solomon summoned him and they brought him from the Altar. Adonijah came and bowed down, honoring the king. Solomon dismissed him, "Go home."

THINK

- Why does it seem that public figures have more than their share of wayward children?
- From what is recorded in the Bible, fewer than half of David's sons "went bad," as they say. Should we be satisfied with such an average? Explain.
- In what ways might David's poor parenting have been the result of his emphasis on other areas of life?
- How does your success rate with your family correlate to the other aspects of your life?
- When it comes to raising your kids, what is success? What temptation is most difficult for you to resist?

PRAY

Lord, give me parenting wisdom to . . .

READ   Life Without Dad

From the *Tri-State Defender* article "Life Without Daddy," by Tim Butler[4]

Do U Know Who Your Daddy Is? is the title of a book from Robert "Pip" Montgomery. As good a question could be—do you know why you do the things you do? According to Montgomery, the reasons we do the things we do in life are connected with our upbringing—or lack of same from an absentee father.

Montgomery told me of a statistic that still rings in his ear: four out of every 10 children in America are living without their father; this means an astonishing 23 million children. He was one of those deprived kids that did not have the nurturing influence of a father during his developing years.

He came to realize that kind of deprivation directly led him to be a womanizer—among other things. Montgomery estimates that by his early 20s he had gone through about 200 women. "I was looking for that attention from my father," he readily admits, "and not only was I destroying myself but I was destroying other women as well."

Just as important, he says, was that those women were drawn to him for the same reasons he was attracted to them. "They were coming to me for the same reasons I was coming to them." They, too, were looking for the attention they missed by not having their fathers around.

THINK

- Play out the statistic that states four of ten children in the U.S. are living without their fathers. What might our society look like in twenty years when these children are becoming parents themselves?
- Why are fathers abdicating their fathering duties in such numbers? What is the pull of this temptation?

- Whether you actually abdicated your family obligations or not, when have you most felt the pull to do just that? What were the circumstances? What were the results of this temptation?

PRAY

Father, help me to never . . .

READ One Game, at Least

From the *Journal of Contemporary Human Services* article "Black Single Custodial Fathers," by Roberta L. Coles[5]

> When I was growing up, I played Little League baseball for three years. My father never attended one game. I'm sorry. In three years you can get away for one game, at least. You know? And he never did. And I asked him to go out and practice with me so I could hit the ball. He bought me a Johnny Batter-Upper so that I could practice by myself. And, you know, it was like that if he was going to the store—hardware store, or anything like that and I might have wanted to go with him, he said, "No, you stay here." It was always like that. . . . So I had been wanting to be a good father for years.

Ephesians 6:4

> Fathers, don't exasperate your children by coming down hard on them. Take them by the hand and lead them in the way of the Master.

THINK

- How likely is it that good fathering impulses of one generation will arise out of bad fathering a generation earlier, as in the first excerpt above?
- The apostle Paul seems to imply that regardless of your marital state, you should raise your children well. Who do you know (it may be yourself) who has indeed raised their children well, despite difficult or even horrific circumstances?
- In what ways do you come down hard on your kids? How would an observer in your home say you exasperate your kids?
- What would it look like to "take [your children] by the hand and lead them in the way of the Master"? How can you do that?

THINK (CONTINUED)

PRAY

God, shape my desires to . . .

READ   The Role of Others

From the *Youthworker Journal* feature "A Word from the Editor," by Tim McLaughlin[6]

It's no secret that parents are the most influential shapers of their children and that the home has the most spiritual influence over kids' spiritual growth. So, reason some leaders in church ministry and Christian education, it stands to reason that youth workers should become change agents primarily among parents, instead of among teenagers. Parents can then become (in the words of one writer) the "primary youth ministers and nurturers of the faith." Another describes it as "a shift from church-centered, home-supported ministry to home-centered, church-supported ministry."

The graduation of my second child from high school gave me cause to ponder my own kids—two of them now in college, one in high school, and another still in elementary school.

And it occurred to me that, however logical and scriptural "family ministry" sounded, I was not directing my own teenagers' spiritual growth anymore.

The thought worried me. So I was a statistic after all, another distant dad who abdicated his spiritual authority in the home—and just when my budding adult children needed my direction the most (judging from everything I had read).

But the more I thought about it, the more distinction I saw between parents as a flagrant spiritual influence, and parents as a flagrant spiritual influence during their children's adolescence. By all means, in early and middle childhood, parents had better lead out in their kids' spiritual formation. But during their adolescence teenagers are differentiating themselves as individuals, as separate entities from the parents—and, of all times in their lives, are most likely to reject or at least sidestep parental influence. The harder parents push, the more their kids tend to react, not conform. Neither is this necessarily rebellion, but simply characteristic adolescent behavior.

For better or worse, the days of my freewheeling spiritual direction of my kids are over. I had my shot when they were younger, when their mother and I made churchgoing a habit for them as it had been for us. In those days they didn't roll their eyes during family Advent readings, didn't sigh when we asked them to pray before a meal. At mealtimes and bedtimes I could read whatever to them, and they enjoyed it—fairy tales, Narnia tales, Old Testament "adventure" stories, episodes from the Gospels. We prayed together—not as much as we should have, and probably not as far into their adolescence as we should have.

They're on their own spiritual paths now. Whatever current spiritual sway I have with my teenagers is incidental and serendipitous. Whatever I tried to sow in them during their younger years about God and his church and spirituality has sprouted differently, unpredictably, perilously in the three of them.

I know I still matter to them, but not as much as I used to. They do listen, however, to other adults they trust—youth workers, coaches, family friends. I am desperately grateful for such adults, grateful that my kids have chosen them as formal or informal confidants. Believe me, I'm banking on the adage that says it takes a village to raise a child.

On the other hand, I realize that a lot of parents are playing catch-up with their teenagers, and are as desperate to connect spiritually with their kids as I am to have "outside" adults connect with mine.

I need other adults for my kids—not because of my busyness or apathy (I hope), but because of where they are developmentally and spiritually. My relationship with God is old hat to them. They want another perspective now. And a patient, interested, interesting, non-parental adult—teacher, youth worker, aunt, uncle, coach—fills a critical role in the spiritual journeys of my nearly adult children.

THINK

- Does this sound like resignation or reality to you? Explain.
- Consider your family for a moment. Was there a time when you all seemed closer to each other than you do now? What was different about that time?
- Is it possible to regain your "lost" or "forgotten" spiritual credibility in the eyes of your kids? How might you do this?
- What is the difference between abdicating parental responsibility and "letting go" of children who want to seek the truth elsewhere? How do you know when the time is right to allow or encourage your kids to connect with their peers or other adults?
- How does it feel when your role in a child's spiritual journey diminishes?

PRAY

Lord, direct me to others who can . . .

LIVE

What I Want to Discuss

What have you discovered this week that you definitely want to discuss with your small group? Write that here. Then begin your small-group discussion with these thoughts.

So What?

Use the following space to summarize the truths you uncovered about the temptation to abdicate your responsibility as a father and how to overcome it. Review your "Beginning Place" if you need to remember where you began. How does God's truth impact the "next step" in your journey?

Then What?

What is one practical thing you can do to apply what you've discovered? Describe how you would put this into practice. What steps would you take? Remember to think realistically—an admirable but unreachable goal is as good as no goal. Discuss your goal in your small group to further define it.

How?

Identify how you will be held accountable to the goal you described. Who will be on your support team? What are their responsibilities? How will you measure the success of your plan? Write the details here.

HOPE

"Leaning, but still standing."

A TIME TO REVIEW

We come to the final lesson in our *Leaning into a Hail of Bullets* discussion guide, but this is not an ending place. Hopefully, you've been discovering some truths about your life and seen opportunity for change—positive change. But no matter what has brought you to lesson 8, know that this is merely a pause in your journey.

You may have uncovered behaviors or thoughts that demanded change. Perhaps you've already changed them. Will the changes stick? How will you continue to take the momentum from this study into next week, next month, and next year? Use this lesson as a time to not only review what you discovered but also determine how you'll stay on track tomorrow.

Talk about your plans with small-group members, commit your plans to prayer, and then do what you say you'll do. As you move forward with a renewed sense of purpose, you'll shrink desperation and grow hope.

READ Temptation to Run from Tough Circumstances

1 Peter 4:12-13,19

Friends, when life gets really difficult, don't jump to the conclusion that God isn't on the job. Instead, be glad that you are in the very thick of what Christ experienced. This is a spiritual refining process, with glory just around the corner. . . .

So if you find life difficult because you're doing what God said, take it in stride. Trust him. He knows what he's doing, and he'll keep on doing it.

THINK

- What from God's Spirit or God's Word can help keep you where you need to be, even in the middle of horrendous circumstances?
- If you're sailing through a smooth stretch of life right now, what can you do to prepare yourself for the inevitable difficulties to come so you will not flee but fight?

PRAY

God, show me . . .

LIVE

- How does God's truth impact the "next step" in your journey?
- How will you get there?
- How will you be held accountable?

READ   Temptation to Drift from Church

Hebrews 10:24-25

> Let's see how inventive we can be in encouraging love and help-
> ing out, not avoiding worshiping together as some do but
> spurring each other on, especially as we see the big Day
> approaching.

THINK

- What aspect of church is (or would be) most likely to drive
  you away?
- What are some inventive ways you can spur on and encourage
  each other and worship together?

PRAY

Lord, challenge me . . .

LIVE

- How does God's truth impact the "next step" in your journey?
- How will you get there?
- How will you be held accountable?

READ Temptation to Fudge on Financials

Romans 13:1,3-4,6-7

Be a good citizen. All governments are under God. Insofar as there is peace and order, it's God's order. So live responsibly as a citizen. . . .

Do you want to be on good terms with the government? Be a responsible citizen and you'll get on just fine, the government working to your advantage. But if you're breaking the rules right and left, watch out. . . .

That's also why you pay taxes—so that an orderly way of life can be maintained. Fulfill your obligations as a citizen. Pay your taxes, pay your bills, respect your leaders.

THINK

- What is your biggest dilemma in the area of finances?
- In what specific ways can your faith affect or change the way you deal with financial responsibilities?

PRAY

God, help me . . .

LIVE

- How does God's truth impact the "next step" in your journey?
- How will you get there?
- How will you be held accountable?

READ Temptation to Follow Lustful Thoughts

1 Corinthians 6:9-12

> Those who use and abuse each other, use and abuse sex, use and abuse the earth and everything in it, don't qualify as citizens in God's kingdom. A number of you know from experience what I'm talking about, for not so long ago you were on that list. Since then, you've been cleaned up and given a fresh start by Jesus, our Master, our Messiah, and by our God present in us, the Spirit.
>
> Just because something is technically legal doesn't mean that it's spiritually appropriate. If I went around doing whatever I thought I could get by with, I'd be a slave to my whims.

THINK

- What habit, behavior, or mindset do you need to change or improve to better avoid lustful thoughts?
- If you've tried before to overcome that temptation, what can you do differently this time in order to be more successful?

PRAY

God, forgive me . . .

LIVE

- How does God's truth impact the "next step" in your journey?
- How will you get there?
- How will you be held accountable?

READ   Temptation to Cheat Your Boss

Proverbs 27:18

> If you care for your orchard, you'll enjoy its fruit;
>> if you honor your boss, you'll be honored.

THINK

- In what ways are you inclined to *not* honor your boss or the company? How might you change that inclination?
- What might it look like to do a better job of honoring your boss or your company?

PRAY

Father, instruct me . . .

LIVE

- How does God's truth impact the "next step" in your journey?
- How will you get there?
- How will you be held accountable?

READ   Temptation to Engage in an Affair

Matthew 5:27-28

You know the next commandment pretty well, too: "Don't go to bed with another's spouse." But don't think you've preserved your virtue simply by staying out of bed.

THINK

- In what ways are you close to investing emotionally or sexually in a woman who is not your wife?
- In what ways can God, God's truth, or other male friends help you defeat this temptation?

PRAY

Lord, guide me . . .

LIVE

- How does God's truth impact the "next step" in your journey?
- How will you get there?
- How will you be held accountable?

READ Temptation to Give Up on Fathering

1 Timothy 3:12-13

> Servants in the church are to be committed to their spouses, attentive to their own children, and diligent in looking after their own affairs. Those who do this servant work will come to be highly respected, a real credit to this Jesus-faith.

THINK

- In what ways do you feel you need to be more committed and attentive to your wife and children?
- With the help of God, what one thing can you do that would move you toward this goal?

PRAY

God, lead me . . .

LIVE

- How does God's truth impact the "next step" in your journey?
- How will you get there?
- How will you be held accountable?

NOTES

INTRODUCTION
1. *Letters of C. S. Lewis* (New York: Harvest/Harcourt, 2003), letter dated January 20, 1942.

LESSON 1
1. Richard Goodall, *The Divorce Dilemma: How Wise Is Today's Received Wisdom* (United Kingdom: Global, 2000), pp. 39, 99-100, 157-158.
2. Jerry White, *Dangers Men Face: Overcoming the Five Greatest Threats to Living Life Well* (Colorado Springs, Colo.: NavPress, 1997), pp. 155-156.

LESSON 2
1. Anne Lamott, *Traveling Mercies: Some Thoughts on Faith* (New York: Anchor/Doubleday, 1999), pp. 99-100.
2. Greg Garrison, "For Many Americans, Church Is Alien Territory," *Religion News Service* (August 29, 1996). Copyright © 1996 Religion News Service. Used by permission.
3. Robert D. Putnam, interview by David J. Wood, in "Let's Meet: Rebuilding Community," *The Christian Century* (February 10, 2004). Copyright © 2004 Christian Century. Reprinted with permission.

LESSON 3
1. "Is It OK to Cheat on Your Taxes?" beliefnet.com (April 16, 2001). This article/poll appeared originally on www.beliefnet.com, "the leading multi-faith website for religion, spirituality, inspiration, and more." Used with permission. All rights reserved.
2. "Cheating on Taxes? Really?!" BookkeeperList.com (January 6, 2004).
3. Frank Lalli, "We're Cheating One Another," *Money* (April 1, 1991).
4. Marcus Borg, "What Belongs to God?" beliefnet.com (April 13, 2000).

LESSON 4

1. Dante Alighieri, *The Divine Comedy: Inferno*, canto 5, trans. Seth Zimmerman.
2. "We've Got Porn," *Christianity Today* (June 12, 2000).
3. Emily Louise Zimbrick, "Looking Beyond Lust," *Washington Times* (November 4, 2003).
4. Pamela Paul, "The Porn Factor," *Time* (January 19, 2004). © 2004 Time, Inc. Reprinted by permission.
5. C. S. Lewis, *The Great Divorce*, pp. 98-101. Copyright © 1959 C. S. Lewis Pte. Ltd. Extracts reprinted by permission.

LESSON 5

1. Dave Simanoff, "An Inside Job," *The Tampa Tribune* (March 31, 2003).
2. Ethics Resource Center, executive summary of the 2003 National Business Ethics Survey, ethics.org.
3. Roberta Maynard, "Leading By Example May Promote Worker Honesty," *Nation's Business* (September 1, 1997).
4. Paul Sloane, "The Temptations of the Web," *Database and Network Journal* (August 1, 2002).

LESSON 6

1. Douglas Young, "Ben," *Between Sundays* (Orono, Maine: Puckerbrush Press, 1978), pp. 29-31.
2. C. S. Lewis, *The Screwtape Letters* (HarperSanFrancisco, 2001), p. 96. Copyright © 1946 C. S. Lewis Pte. Ltd.
3. (Name withheld), "Readers Write," *The Sun* (March 2004).
4. Janet Reibstein and Martin Richards, *Sexual Arrangements: Marriage and the Temptation of Infidelity* (New York: Scribners, 1993).
5. Camille Chatterjee, "Overcoming Sex: Can Men and Women Be Friends?" *Psychology Today* (September 1, 2001).

LESSON 7

1. David Popenoe, *Life Without Father: Compelling New Evidence That Fatherhood and Marriage Are Indispensable for the Good of Children and Society* (New York: The Free Press, 1996).
2. Peggy O'Mara, "Who's in Charge?" *Mothering* (March 22, 1989).
3. Jean Torkelson, "Coach's 'Abuse' of Wife Spawned Promise Keepers," *Rocky Mountain News* (October 5, 1997).
4. Tim Butler, "Life Without Daddy," *Tri-State Defender* (December 24, 2003).
5. Roberta L. Coles, "Black Single Custodial Fathers: Factors Influencing the Decision to Parent," *Families in Society: The Journal of Contemporary Human Services* (April 1, 2003). Reprinted with permission from Families in Society (www.familiesinsociety.org), published by the Alliance for Children and Families.
6. Tim McLaughlin, "A Word from the Editor," *Youthworker Journal* (Fall 1995).

ANOTHER "PULL-NO-PUNCHES" HONEST DIALOGUE ABOUT THE ISSUES THAT MATTER MOST TO MEN.

Treading Water in an Empty Pool

You can regain hope and purpose in what seems to be your out-of-control life. Tackle disappointment and unease by exploring useful spiritual principles from movies, literature, pop culture, and especially God's Word in the easy-to-understand language of *The Message*.

The Navigators
1-57683-689-4

Perfect companion to the REAL LIFE STUFF FOR MEN series.

The Message

All sixty-six books of the *Message* Bible are conveniently combined into one. From the mysterious Old Testament stories to the straightforward teachings of Jesus to the encouraging early church letters, reading *The Message* will jump-start your heart, challenge your mind, and forever change your life.

Eugene H. Peterson
1-57683-289-9

To order copies, visit your local Christian bookstore,
call NavPress at 1-800-366-7788,
or log on to www.navpress.com.

To locate a Christian bookstore near you,
call 1-800-991-7747.

BRINGING TRUTH TO LIFE
www.navpress.com